I0113737

SITUATED SEX
&
KNOWER

(Sexual Imprint For Common + LBGTQ+)

Professor Imad Fawzi Shueibi

Introduction

Every person in this world in a distinctive imprint; i.e., they have their unique unmatched personality. This definitely means that there are serious disparities between the types of thinking of males and females in addition to qualitative biological differences between the two sexes. Males and females are different type each; they may be visual, auditory, kinesthetic or olfactory. However, it happens that some people might have more than one distinctive characteristic. Those are the people who are the most difficult to deal with. Everyone of them is a situated knower and has their innate distinctive characteristics that make them a unique entity.

These disparities are not only social or cultural; they are cognitive and biological. That is why there are differences which might be sharp between males and females. There are even differences between males themselves and females themselves. They mainly centre round misunderstanding between the two sexes, having different ways of thinking, different behavior … etc. You must bear in mind, dear reader, that those disparities will result in a kind of diversity which manifests in acquiring knowledge, having different levels of sexual desire and even different sexual practice (**situated sex**), and reaching the very results in different ways. In other words, each sex has their own way of obtaining the very piece of knowledge, dealing with it, processing it, comprehending it or transferring it. This is, in fact, the bless we have been endowed with. Has all mankind had the same way of thinking and the same tastes, everyone on earth would be no more than a replica of the other.

Everyone has their own way of reaching the same point. That is true, but sometimes the person's own way may lead to a different result in non-general issues such as addition and mathematics due to the fact that different ways of thinking lead to different outcomes. This explains why human beings have different ideas, convictions and values, let alone the differences in evaluating others and respecting or violating their rights. This way also indicates the different kinds of interest people have. Some people highly concentrate on their body, others on ideas and some have interest in both; body and ideas, in different proportions. People, in general, do not have the same level of cognition because they are different "*situated knowers*"; thus, they have their own way of acquiring knowledge, as we already said.

In the light of the abovementioned, we must think deeply and work hard to reach common grounds on which to build our understanding of one another whether we are males or females.

> *In the early beginnings of your relationship with any female, you have to avoid insisting on knowing everything about her.*

Males and Females As "Situated Knowers"

We are a mixture world combining male and female together. Do we not have both hormones; masculine and feminine, regardless of whether we are males or females? Is not the word "androgen" derived from "pine" which combines both; male and female genitals, and is self-pollinating? This means it can turn into a male and a female, and so is the hormone of androgen.

Accept the female as a situated knower to win her. Avoid negating her. The moment you try to change the female's way of thinking or behavior, you begin to lose her. This will manifest itself in her fury at you and will end with her leaving you

Hence, we are males and females at the same time as far as our minds are concerned. The following example will help simplify this idea: Let us consider that a male embryo is XY (notice here that the chromosomal structure consists of a male Y and a female X) and let us suppose that it needs one unit of the male sex hormone to be able to make male sexual organs, and three units, for example, to be able to form the main masculine encephalic operating system. But, due to some reasons, the embryo does not receive the prerequisite amount; i.e., if the embryo needs four units and it only gets three, then one unit would be directed towards forming the sexual organs, and only two will be left to form the brain. This means that the brain would be 2/3 masculine (and 1/3 feminine). This would result in a baby who would, later, have a masculine mind, yet s/he will still enjoy feminine thinking and characteristics. (These are virtual proportions).

> Hatred is an expression of your inability to love, not because the other deserves this. Learn not to inhibit yourself before reaching the point of hatred.

The other possibility is that the embryo receives only two units of hormones; one of which would be dedicated to forming the testicles, but the brain would be under the effect of one unit; a process that would result in a genetically male baby with a femininely-formed brain, and basically feminine thinking. When this baby reaches the phase of puberty, there would be a possibility for him/her to become sexually abnormal. When the embryo is feminine, there would be a few or no male hormones in it. This means that the sexual organs are feminine and the main brain structure would maintain its feminine characteristics. The brain would continue to receive feminine hormones and would develop all the qualities necessary for building "the nest" and protecting it, in addition to building the centres necessary for deciphering verbal and non-verbal signals.

> Do not ever meet your female without offering her something that relates to feelings.

When this baby comes out to the world, its external appearance would be feminine as well as its behavior due to encephalic data. However, sometimes, in a way that has not previously been planned, the embryo may receive a sudden portion of male sex hormones. In this case, the baby will come out to the world with a clearly masculine appearance.

It is believed that 80 – 85% of men basically have masculine encephalic data, and that 15–20 % of them have a feminine brain. Many men who belong to the second group would become sexually deviants in the phase of puberty. It worth mentioning that 15 – 20 % of men have a feminine brain, while only 10 % of women have a masculine brain.

We have to bear in mind that the psychological conditions a pregnant woman goes through would allow for an increase or a shortage of masculine or feminine hormones in her body. These hormones, in turn, reach the embryo during mitosis and during the formation of its brain. This means that any malfunction would affect the embryo and the way of thinking s/he will have in the future.

When we talk about the female sex in this book, we are but confining ourselves to dealing with about 90% of females who are programmed by feminine patterns of behavior. The remaining 10% of females have a brain which has, in a way or another, different masculine abilities. This is due to the fact that between the sixth and the eighth weeks after fertilization, the embryo would receive a portion of male hormones.

When we disagree with our peers, our cerebral and psychological, and consequently, our chemical conditions will be a major cause of the problems that arise between us.

Certainly, we are not always responsible for our conflict nor are we responsible for our understanding of one another; simply because we are subject to our biological and hormonal cycles. When we are in a state of harmony with our partners, our cerebrums secrete two chemicals that evoke a number of feelings; phenylethylamine (PEA) and noradrenalin.

Phenylethylamine is a natural amphetamine that betters one's temperament. Secretion of the PEA urges the secretion of dopamine which evokes the positive function of neuro-conductor between the two cerebral hemispheres; a case that will, inevitably lead to comprehending each other and feeling one another.

PEA increases cell connectivity and explains the reason behind our clear thinking in the early morning though we stayed late the night before talking to the one we love. Production of this substance prevents the masculine hemisphere from dominating our cerebrums and incites the right hemisphere to work. It should be noted that it is our right cerebrum that is responsible for the feelings of beauty, relaxation, love, under-   standing and comprehension. This means that lack of production of this substance prevents us from listening to each other and prevents the feminine hemisphere from providing us with creative techniques to solve our problems of misunderstanding. It is worth mentioning here that there is a strong relation between the feeling of happiness and the PEA which is a chemical our bodies release in some cases such as eating a piece of chocolate.

This substance, however, is a strong stimulant that has a completely opposite impact to its value on understanding. It is one of the reasons why we suffer from tension in the early weeks of any emotional relationship. We might suffer from stomach-ache or we might mistakenly think that we will be in a state of nausea upon seeing the person we love.

The other chemical released by our cerebrums when we are in a state of understanding or love is the noradrenalin which is closely associated with the sense of contingency.

It is one of the neuro-conductors that are responsible for palm sweating, raising blood pressure and heartbeat rate. It is also responsible for our sense of happiness and activity as well as our intensive concentration on the one we love. Therefore, it is used in the production of some medicines of anti-depression and anti-anxiety though this chemical is released during sharp fits of anxiety or rage.

When we fall in love or enjoy a state of harmony, there is another chemical secreted in the body but not much; it is the serotonin which is released in small amounts in the abovementioned cases and in cases of depression.

> *Do not count on the surface meaning of the female's words. Go far beyond. You should nourish her femininity with appropriate caring. If she tries to tell you how people complimented her, she is not arousing your jealousy, she does not care for all admirers even though this issue is highly important for her. She is looking for emotional boost.*

There are some similarities between a person experiencing love and a person undergoing compulsory obsession. In this case, we have to realize that decrease of the serotonin levels is the cause of the state of lack of happiness that we feel; a state that is contrary to love, but this gives an explanation why love is accompanied with happiness and depression alike. Thus, we come to notice the neural, hormonal and psychological contradiction we all have and which indicates that we need phenylethylamine, noradrenalin and serotonin to be happier, more understanding and to be in good terms with those around us.

An infatuated lover speaking about the positive characteristics of his beloved is the best example of the low levels of the serotonin in particular which influences our concentration and coercive interest. This dysfunctions the frontal lobe that is responsible for sound judgement, and here arises the following question: Does our ability to have good judgment become dysfunctional when we love or quarrel? The answer manifests in the low serotonin levels that incapacitate the frontal lobe and the secretion of adrenaline during outrage.

When we are in a state of love, our minds fall short of realizing the demerits of those we love. The natural abilities that we seek the help of to evaluate others within a social framework paralyze when we look at the person we love. What happens is that such neural circles are not charged; therefore, they stop working. Low serotonin levels give the reason behind the state of blindness that afflicts lovers, but it enhances their relationship since the part of the cerebrum that is responsible for passing judgments was disabled. Researches in this field indicate that low serotonin levels also give an explanation for our premonitions and our sense of insecurity.In a word, we are subject to the paradox of gaining the happiness of love, yet losing sound judgement which we also lose when we get angry or sad. Hence, it is up to us to choose love or anger and sadness!

> *Females do not speak directly about their matters. They beat about the bush and they often use the fuzzy logic. That is why most women enjoy it when men describe them as butterflies.*

Male and Female:
Two Creatures ... Two Worlds

"You just do not understand" is a phrase commonly used by parties in conflict. It is the most flagrant description of the disparity of two different creatures despite all the attempts made by Gender theoreticians to make society appear to be the reason behind all differences between males and females. In fact, that has not been approved by modern and contemporary scientific studies at all.

"You just don't understand" is not a problem of dialogue between two different creatures; it is a problem of everything; a problem of body language, problem-voicing language, language of sympathy, language of hatred, language of communication ... etc. In brief, male and female are only two creatures who accidentally met on a planet called "Earth".

Those creatures produce "androgen"; the bisexual hormone that produces masculine and feminine hormones. Each one of them exists in the other and has the other inside them; i.e., everyone has masculine and feminine hemispheres in addition to the animus and anima. The animus is the masculine spirit that exists in the left hemisphere of the cerebrum, and the anima is the feminine spirit that exists in the right hemisphere. These two do actually create two worlds which unity needs a special craft. Here, the male has to exercise his right hemisphere to understand the female, and the female needs to exercise her left hemisphere to understand the male. Both, the male and female truly need to understand and comprehend the other so as to create links between their different worlds.

D. Kimora (1989-1999; Butler 1988) believes that men and women share the very genetic material, except for the two sex chromosomes. The differences between men and women come as

11

a result of the different hormones affecting the brain during its formation. Thus, sex differentiation begins.

At the early stages of life, estrogen (the female sex hormone) and androgen, especially testosterone (the male sex hormone), work effectively ever since the embryonic phase where each living mammal, including humans, has the potential to be a male or female. If the embryo carries the chromosome Y, then the first step towards masculinization lies in the formation of the two masculine gonads (the testicles). Thus, secretion of male hormones begins. But, if the two gonads do not secrete male hormones or, for some reason, these hormones could not affect the tissue, then this human being will be a female.

> *Do not get provoked or irritated if your female raises any illogical issue. Think it out by using your feeling and intuition and you will discover that such an issue really has positive ideas. Get rid of the ideas which do not relate to the actual reality and think positively of the female's ideas.*

When the testicles are formed, they secrete two substances that lead to masculinity of the embryo in the uterus. Those two substances are the Testosterone and the Mullerian Regression Hormone (MRH).

Kimora believes that male hormones not only cause the genitals to be male organs, but they are also responsible for regulating the masculine behavior at an early stage of life, and for determining the process of cognition of males and females.

Kimora has inferred this fact by noticing that the cerebral spot responsible for regulation or what is called "the hypothalamus", which is situated above the endocrine pituitary gland, is bigger in males' brains than in females'.

Hence, Kimora believes that due to being exposed to sex hormones at early stages of life, cerebral changes that affect the human being for their whole life occur. She identifies the problem cognitively as a differentiation between both sexes ever since the formation moment in the uterus. This never changes by time or by being exposed to hormonal changes after parturition.

> Since the female likes the *"shadow & light" game*, she does not plainly express her ideas. She demands you of guessing what they are, and would be very upset if you do not know them and would contempt deep inside her not realizing her symbols and signs.

Another study conducted by another scholar called Lofay from Salk Institute of Biological Studies reveals that the frontal part of the hypothalamus of males is bigger than that of females and it is smaller in homosexual men than in heterosexual men. This part exists in females and is similar to the part that homosexuals have. Therefore, the homosexual description has changed today into having a certain sexual situation; they have a biological reason.

Cognitive and Biological Differences between Males & Females

Many prominent scientists (such as Kimora 1989-1999; Butler 1988; Berton and Levy 1989; McGinnis 1976; Ellen and Gorski 1991; Anki 1992; Driessen 1995; and Beckenberg and Johnson 1997) noticed the differences in the cerebrum size between males and females. hese disparities and structural differences could be the reason of the differences of behavior, growth and cognitive comprehension between males and females.

Studies show that the cerebrum of males is 10-15% bigger than that of females and is 100g heavier (Anki 1992). Moreover, men have a billion neurons more in the cortex cerebri than women (Beckenberg & Gonderson 1997).

Leave the floor to your female to talk. She cannot survive without using her ultimate means of the audio communication, whether by talking to you or to others, or by listening to you talking. You should realize that you cannot match her ability to talk, and that she needs four times your oral and audio capacities.

Other differences can be spotted in the subthalamus of females which contains smaller or bigger areas if compared to that of males. These areas are (INAH) and (SCN). The former plays a very important role in reproduction and the latter in the biological rhythms. Neuroanatomists and growth specialists have found out that during the early years of one's life up to the age of five, the rate of cerebrum growth differs within the very sex, whether male or female, and between the two sexes. This is the reason which some specialists attributed to the superiority of males in spatial tasks and the superiority of females in performing tasks related to language, speaking and reading in childhood. There are, definitely, other functional differences between males and females that we will deal with.

In general, females surpass males in performing the following tasks and skills:

1. *Skills of finger moving; moving fingers fast and harmoniously.*
2. *Math and computer tests.*
3. *Performing several tasks at a time.*
4. *Remembering places of things in a particular order.*
5. *Spelling.*
6. *Fluency at using words.*
7. *Tasks that need sensitivity towards external stimulants (except for visual females).*
8. *Remembering signs all along the road.*
9. *Exercising verbal memory.*
10. *Depth estimation and quick perception.*
11. *Understanding body language and facial expressions.*

Males, on the other hand, surpass females in performing the following tasks and skills:

1. *Skills of shooting.*
2. *Using Vocabulary.*
3. *Long-time concentrations.*
4. *Mathematical thinking and problem solving.*
5. *Navigation and good-consideration of the geometric features of places.*
6. *Verbal intelligence.*
7. *Creating and persevering habits.*
8. *Most spatial tasks.*

When talking to a female, slow down before responding; i.e., absorb and represent her. Use her own way of thinking. Do not use your ideas. This requires you, as a male, to hold back responses.

Some other studies find out that there are girls who are more boyish and aggressive than their sisters. This is because they were exposed to large amounts of androgen during pregnancy. They also preferred boys' games.

Thus, females who are exposed, while in their mother's uteruses, to higher androgen levels are deeply affected, especially as regards "spatial performance". But, the relation is not linear because spatial abilities do not increase with the increase of androgens. Kimora's study points out that men with low testosterone levels are superior to those with high-testosterone-levels in spatial tests. It also points out that women with high testosterone levels are better than those with low testosterone levels. These results reflect that there is an ideal level of androgens where spatial performance can be the best; the level lies within the minimum limits in the case of males.

One would be dazzled whenever they hear males and females talking to each other. This makes us wonder about the way they talk; how one sex member asks about something and gets answers, from the opposite sex, that show complete irrelevance to what they are asking about. This clearly reflects the sharp differences between males and females; differences in cognition and biology though there are theories that insist on the idea that social experience can moderate biological differences between the two sexes since the latter; i.e., males and females, are supposed to be equal in their abilities and thinking in a way that biology cannot recognize.

> Receiving lovely words and feelings are a priority in a female's life on condition that she is not deceived. The feeling of being deceived will arouse a feeling of inferiority. This can only be avoided by joining words and deeds.

The male's way of expressing himself is structurally — not socially — different from that of the female. Some societies, for instance, prevent males from expressing their feelings and, sometimes, they make the language of males relatively void of any emotional expression. Such societies might not succeed in making all males clones of one another especially in the case of male artists, poets, and intuitionists whose nature manifests itself with no regard whatsoever to society. Parallelistically, such societies cannot teach the female how to express her needs indirectly since they only have this structural way of expression.

Approving the male's behavior, decisions and ambitions is the best way to his heart, for a male likes it when a spade is called a spade. He would, furthermore, like to enjoy serenity when accompanied by his female. Female, on the other hand, certainly likes the male who expresses his feelings in a direct way. Yet, she does not prefer the direct way of expressing her own love and thoughts. She might do this every now and then especially if she is an auditory female because such a type listens and speaks at the same time, yet they prefer using symbols. Thus, males and females simply think in two different ways because they use two different hemispheres.

There is another difference as far as their minds are concerned. Male's mind is competitive and it follows a hierarchy where there is always a head and followers, whereas a female thinks in a communicative circular way where there is no ultimate value for competition or for the top of the hierarchy. What concerns the female is what goes beyond the achievement, and what effect the latter is going to have on her own and her male's feelings. In other words, she is not concerned with things themselves. She is, rather, concerned with how these things are going to affect her emotionally.

It should be noted that, socially-speaking, there are some women who would like to be liberated. Those find it convenient and satisfying to be described as men-like and that they have the ability to work and comprehend things like men do. Though this notion was intended to put an end to the prejudice and injustice practiced over women, it, however, enforced such prejudice due to referential comparison to men. Actually, such a case deprives the female from having her own entity. Therefore, conflicts arise between both sexes since females would try hard to prove their existence and independence. Not only this, they would also suffer from unstable relationship that may end in divorce, if they are married, or it may up in breaking up, if they are not, no matter how much they love one another.

> When a female lies,she does not always have sinister intentions. Her lying is a kind of harmonizing with the nature of her prevaricative mind.

The Exceptional Nature of LGBTQ+

The LGBTQ+ are normal people and belong to the exceptional percentage of 2.5% of the world population. They enjoy a different cerebral nature which makes their sexual tendencies different from the rest of the people who constitute 83.67%. However, the remaining 12.83% of people share the LBGTQ+ their special homosexual tendencies.

The hypothalamus and hippocampus are the parts that determine the sexual nature and orientation. It is quite known that this area is bigger in males than in females and this size is attributed to the amount of the sexual hormone (estrogen and testosterone) a fetus gets while in their mother's womb. When a female fetus receives a bigger potion of estrogen than normal, the hypothalamus and hippocampus get smaller; therefore, she would have greater sexual desire than her peers and she would tend to be lesbian. It is good to know that lesbianism is divided into 16 different degrees, the lowest of all may be admiration in a woman and her femininity, going up towards desiring in another woman (woman/woman) and not ending in a man-woman desiring a woman, in which case a woman acts like a man in sex. In facts, degrees of lesbianism are numerous and differ completely from man/man orientation. This is because a female is enjoys a more creative and diverse sexual nature than man.

As for men, if they receive a big potion of estrogen while in their mother's womb, their hypothalamus and hippocampus will get smaller than in the majority of men. This leads to an anal fixation in males and they become passive in sex; i.e., they will be acted upon. However, when the estrogen and testosterone rates are equal, the sexual orientation will oscillate equally between being sexually active or passive. That is why the masculine homosexuality is no more than five degrees.

1. An active man with a passive man, with no desire in women.

2. An active/passive man with an active/passive, with no desire in women.

3. A passive man with a passive man, something like lesbianism but in a formal way.

4. An active man with a passive man, but both could have a desire in women.

5. An active/passive man with an active/passive man (bisexual), with a desire in woman.

This category who enjoys such a sexual diversity is different from the average people who constitute 83.67%, and have a different way of thinking.

Passive men have high intuition and cognitively psychic abilities, but they do not excel at Math which females (who are sexually active) excel at.

It should be noted that when we use the terms (active) and (passive), we are denoting sexual tendencies which – scientifically – cannnot be subject to any value judgments; i.e., they are neither positive nor negative. This, rather, implies the tendencies which please this party or that, which is something to respect and enact protective governmental laws for. Their rights should be admitted without any convictions or application of the common knowledge or religious and cognitive fallacies.

The exceptionality of such people is what describes them best as they are different and normal; they are not abnormal in any case. It should be noted that abnormality could be defined as going against your nature, and such people are not going against their own natures.

For more information, you can download this application (Doctor X) from Google Play and take the relevant tests that illuminate subscribers about their sexual nature and identity:

https://play.google.com/store/apps/details?id=com.application.doctorx

To conclude, what applies to females in this book, applies to the passive kind of LGBTQ+. That is why reading the book would benefit them a lot.

Situated Sex!

Males and females do not only have biological differences; they also have different ways of accessing knowledge. This is associated to the differences of the sexual nature of either sex; i.e., as male or female.

The hormones a fetus gets at the mitosis phase, while in the uterus, lead to a difference in the nature of the two cerebral hemispheres that change the nature of the sexual act of the male and female. As the right and left cerebral hemispheres vary according to symmetrical and non-symmetrical fission mechanism that gives the cerebrum its unique imprint, the cornu ammonis (hippocampus) and hypothalamus determine the unique imprint nature of both sexes and the organ of each sex.

According to some research conducted in this field, scientists say that women have a smaller size of hippocampus compared to men, and so do homosexual men have. They also have a smaller hippocampus than average men.

There are some preliminary studies that speak about the different measurements of hippocampus between a male and a male, and a female and a female. Those studies reveal the complexity of the mitosis phase and the complexities that afflict the cerebrum in consequence. This, in fact, gives every human being their unique and particular sexual imprint.

The hypothalamus is the residence place of the (autonomic nervous system) while the hippocampus is the main part responsible for the formation of the special events and the linkage between these events and their contexts. The latter; i.e., the hippocampus, sends the receptors that enable it to respond to hormones. Lately, it has been noticed that it atrophies in case of undergoing sexual and psychological disorders, which clearly indicates its role in the sexual process. It imparts sentiments and affections on any piece of information acquired since it closely relates to the limpic nervous system which is responsible for sex and emotion. Thus, it controls everything that relates the sexual behavior; a process that happens in cooperation with the amygdala.

* * * * * *

Differences of Feelings

There is no doubt whatsoever that there are qualitative differences in the feelings of males and females as far as desire and orgasm are concerned. In fact, this is the difference between male and female as situated sexes. It is worth mentioning that what gets a high importance in this regard is the qualitative differences between members of the same sex and the male and female sexual body map, or rather their erogenous zones.

No male resembles the other as related to desire, sexual body map or the peak of orgasm. This explains the disharmony between partners; disharmony that might reach the extent of psychological and physical divorce.

Differences of bodies do not have to do only with sex which nature already differs between male and female. In other words, there are disparities between the biological, hormonal and anatomical natures between male and female. Nonetheless, this issue gets more complicated if we get into its details. Let us take the female as an example:

From the perspective of sexual anatomy, women are three categories: clitoral, vaginal and blended. This classification is not adequate if we are to determine the sexual nature of a female because the geography of pleasure or the sexual map of her body may reside in zones the male may not pay attention to due to his stereotypical behaviour with his female partner.

This means that pleasure can fix in several places of women's bodies else than the female genital organ. These zones can be: (see the figure)

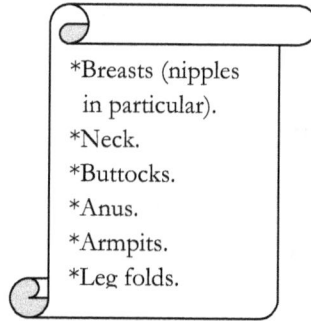

*Breasts (nipples
in particular).
*Neck.
*Buttocks.
*Anus.
*Armpits.
*Leg folds.

These zones might be related to early sexual experiences a person might have undergone. Therefore, they appear to be conditioned. Nevertheless, this cannot determine the bodily sexual map or the geography of pleasure properly because the same experiences may not lead to the same conditioning or the same sexual pleasure in the case of those who underwent sexual experiences that had similar conditions.

We sometimes consider the geography of pleasure as having two factors; situated sex and the socio-sexual interactions. The first factor is a decisive one due to the unique cognitive and sexual cerebral nature of every human being. The second factor has to do with the way these interactions emerge in the life of every individual. To put it differently, the consequences of sexual pleasure or sexual bruises that result from sexual experiences in one's early childhood always appear as binary associations (situated sex – experience). There will not be any similar consequences unless there is similarity in the situated sex.

In brief, symptoms and manifestations of psycho-sexual ailments are not the same. They are as different as people's feelings and desires are.

Never have the illusion that you are required to be in a predicatory or a disciplinary mission. This is the first lesson to be learned: **"You have your own character and she has her own"**. Each of your "situated knowers" has already been formed. You should bear in mind that your relationship with a female is based on accepting the other. You are not an executioner or a creator to recreate her, nor is she. Therefore, **you should accept her as she is**.

* * * * *

Back to speak about disparities. Some people might have the pleasure of looking, listening, touching, smelling or any other sense-related pleasure. Some of them might combine more than one kind. We cannot,   however, regard this phenomenon as libidinous fixation, according to psycho-analysis, nor can we regard it as conditioning, according to behavioral psychology. This is, in fact, what we call situated sex" which cannot be attributed to one reason (in a linear way); rather, it forms depending on the sexual nature of cerebrum, the experiences attributed to this nature and the positive and negative consequences of such experiences. Therefore, a healthy sexual meeting will be a meeting in which both parties have or almost have the very sexual nature, as situated sexes.

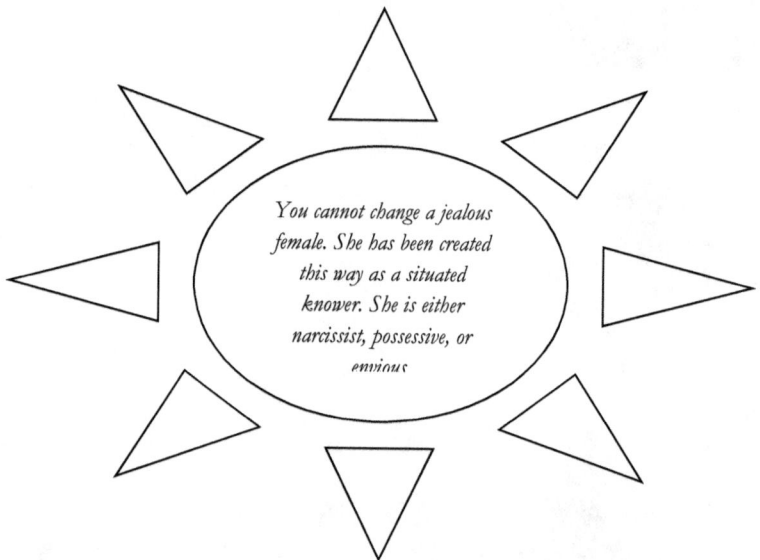

You cannot change a jealous female. She has been created this way as a situated knower. She is either narcissist, possessive, or envious

It is good to know that an auditory female will not lead a healthy sexual life without having her sense of hearing enhanced. A visual female, on the other hand, will never like it to live in the dark with nothing to see. Similarly, if a kinesthetic female does not deal with her body and her partner's body in a proper active way, she will consider herself performing a social role when making love, no more, since it does not conform to her body nature and structure. So is the male, but with some differences.

In a nutshell, it is situated sex that uncovers the reality of life diversity. It is the best indicator of the richness of the lives of people. This, actually, raises a very crucial question: How could people coexist if the possibilities of meeting a partner, who has almost similar situated sex, are at a minimum? Indeed, this issue is like a game of dice for it raises a question about the identity of that human being who can adapt to another creature who has slight resemblance to, with a minimum probability.

Such questions require writing another book to be answered in full and to be given the proper attention. Be sure, dear reader, you are not going to wait for long to dive into the deep ocean of self-knowledge and pick the jewels you have always dreamt of obtaining.

* * * * *

> Male is different from female in view of the fact that his unloading of emotion could be attained through sex.

Are Hormones and Conflicts Related?

Although love and conflict have to do with affection, feelings and mind, we must always remember that there are chemical, physiological and hormonal factors which could be signs or indicators that might lead us to understand how human relationships work.

Once we understand this chemical hormonal factor in human relationships, we can, at a later stage, use it to control our hormones so as to actually lay the bases for a better life. Such understanding would act as if it were a paved road or a ploughed land that would render abundance of fruits. In fact, understanding the role of this chemical hormonal factor will help create a different situation between male and female.

Understanding the conflict between male and female would help them drain, decrease or narrow this conflict down. This can certainly be a result of dealing with hormones either positively or negatively.

There is no direct linear relation between hormones and human behavior. However, if this relation is considered to be related to different factors, hormones, herein, play a vital role. We can, at least, deal with one factor; therefore, we can develop a more positive behavior between the male and female so as to make understanding the problem easier.

This gives the opportunity to deal with other factors such as the nature of thinking, feelings and convictions. It enables us, as well, to develop a positive relationship with the other. But, if we fail in dealing with them, the relationship will turn into a negative state.

In this regard, we can say that some specialized glands secrete those hormones which flow in our blood and act as lubricants, metaphorically speaking, or incentives for our lives.

Cholesterol and adrenaline, for instance, are hormones secreted by the suprarenal gland and they have extremely important functions. The Adrenaline, accompanied by cholesterol, provides the body with a high level of energy for raising the ability of self-defense. Thus, those hormones are released at moments of fury, fear, or facing awkward situations.

As soon as cholesterol and adrenaline are produced, the body stops, delays or decreases the usual functions of some parts to a minimum.

When we are scared, alert, angry, or ready to fight, we do not feel hungry, but this is not always good. Although those hormones help us face and adapt to a variety of difficult situations, they damage our immunity and digestion systems because they are not supposed to last forever, and so is love.

> *Do not blame the female at the time she is undergoing a masculine situation. Try to treat her sentimentally to help her restore the feminine side of her personality, and encourage her to spend some time out with other females. This will revive her*

Even when we undergo long periods of (psychological) pressure or when we come into collision with our partners, we find that the hormones which increased at the beginning to address the problem or tragedy soon decreased because their existence is illogical; i.e., the continuous secretion of such hormones is not reasonable at all, on the one hand. On the other hand, their existence in blood is likely to cause unbearable states that could be regarded as serious or excessive, such as tension, anxiety and high blood pressure. Such states lead to what we metaphorically ca "cocooning" where one indulges themselves with their problem to the extent of addiction or danger.

Gradually the body starts to give up, for the glands canno continue to produce such hormones if the problematic situatior the state of danger which a person is undergoing or the conflic between male and female continues.

We all know that hormones affect the sugar rates in bloo and make them unstable. This also affects one's temperament tha will often be mercurial. In such a case, there will be two differen effects on both sexes due to the secretion of cholesterol anc adrenaline. One of them manifests in the male's tendency tc neglect his female. This will result in the subsidence of hi emotional and sexual desire; a situation that makes the female star to get tired of those hormones, so she, or rather her body, tries tc get rid of them as soon as possible. It should be noted that in the case of females, this process of hormone ridding takes a shorte time than in the case of males. But, in the course of time, the female gets overwhelmed by the feeling that the male does not care for her till she falls a victim for acute frustration.

It is noticeable that rise in the cholesterol rates soon shows on the female's body; it, very rapidly, accumulates fat in her body and she will clearly be overweight especially if she is suffering from tension or is in a state of disharmony with her partner. This state is quite similar to the state of the female who undergoes the menopause where she produces weak estrogen that comes to be stored as fat.

As time goes by, the female's weight increases, she feels dissatisfied with her body and she soon gets into what could be called as "*a bad circle*". Therefore, she begins to suffer from anxiety, on the one hand, and from her male's inattention, on the other hand. This accumulates more fat and aggravates her worry over her body that is no longer the body she used to have; a situation that gives her the feeling that she will not be accepted by her male anymore and will, again, have a negative impact on her.

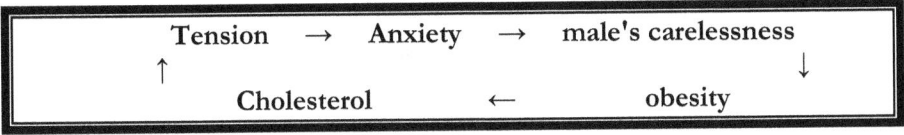

Tension	→	Anxiety	→	male's carelessness
↑				↓
	Cholesterol		←	obesity

Adrenaline and cholesterol stir up the release of insulin which rouses the stomach to demand more food. In this case, we have either of two possibilities: either a rise in sugar rates which results in diabetes or gaining more weight. It is worth mentioning here that anxiety badly affects the body and leads to diabetes. There are other possibilities that manifest in having a range of ailments caused by the over-rise of cholesterol, adrenaline and insulin.

The conflict between male and female leads to a number of health problems and their consequences such as indulging and enveloping oneself in a circle of conflicts, illnesses and hopeless cases. We have to learn that the conflict between the male and female lies in the fact that they have different body reactions when they experience the severe stings of conflict.

When in conflict, females' bodies release quite big amounts of cholesterol while males' bodies release much fewer amounts. Cholesterol rise in the female's body soon burns carbohydrates instead of fat, thus lactic acid results and makes the female feel tiredness and fatigue because muscles quickly get affected. This case is like what one feels when they do not practice sports continuously. So, production of lactic acid makes them feel extremely sore muscles. The female goes through the experience of producing lactic acid which renders dire consequences. This process gradually, yet quickly, destroys calcium in the body and results in osteoporosis. That is why 80–90% of those who suffer from osteoporosis are females.

Contrariwise, when the testosterone levels go up in the male's body, he begins to regain his interest in the female who becomes happier and more serene, and she gets more attracted to her partner.

The equation, then, is that simple: in case of love and attraction, bodies of each of the male and female, secrete a special hormone which in turn motivates the hormone of the other. At the beginning, testosterone stimulates oxytocin in the female's body, and the oxytocin motivates the female to feel her femininity and her male's care. In response, the female sends the male a positive sensation of interaction, so testosterone levels increase in his body, and they both get into a positive circle. Anyhow, you have to bear in mind, dear reader, that it is the male who should take the initiative, in the first place.

When conflict breaks out between male and female, testosterone levels go down in the male's body, thus he loses interest in his female. It is good to know that a male can actually show care for his female when he is in a state of high concentration on her or if he is not in a state of mental distraction. However, as soon as the female feels the male's care, she shows him similar care. In fact, both of them motivate the other's hormones.

When the male stops caring for his female because of business or nuisance resulting from conflict with her,

he will have low testosterone levels and she will have low oxytocin levels. They will, consequently, get back to the bad (vicious) circle we have already talked about.

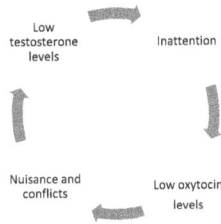

When the female feels neglected, she starts to make life unpleasant as an expression of resentment which again decreases testosterone in her male's body.

Success in life, work, love, etc, increases the production of testosterone in the male's body, but as for those who did not achieve success in their lives, they suffer from low testosterone levels. That is why depressed men do not think of sex nor do women. In addition, they usually suffer from the lack of the masculinity hormone; i.e., testosterone.

We also notice that businessmen who orbit the world of money, those who work day and night, or those who work in politics do not, any longer, care for the female because the testosterone levels have decreased in their bodies.

The more harmonious the male with his female is, the abler he will be to produce testosterone. He, subsequently, stimulates the female to produce oxytocin. Contrariwise, the more anxious he is, the less testosterone he produces.

Therefore, the male and female, definitely, need a weekly, perhaps a monthly, or, certainly, a yearly vacation in order to reproduce these hormones in a better and more positive way.

It is worth mentioning here that the hormone of masculinity increases at the beginning of the day. However, the male consumes it during daytime work. After sunset, the male feels he no longer has sufficient hormones to communicate love. In fact, this is the very time at which the female needs serious care and stimulation of oxytocin in her body.

When the sexual intercourse comes in the evening after a hectic day, it will not match aspirations. Sometimes it seems to be routinous and it lacks the sufficient stimulation of oxytocin that adds splendor and beauty to this relationship as well as more estrogen in the male's body. Thus, routine, depression, boredom and monotony dominate lives of the male and female.

Low testosterone levels manifest in many cases like: fidgety, fury, fluctuating temperament, inattention and carelessness. The male feels that he needs attention to get motivated, therefore, he demands his female partner to care and look after him. He wants her to be his mother at this moment. The female, very often, refrains from giving him anything because she waits for him to start caring for her so as to return it (times doubled). Unfortunately, such a case makes conflict aggravates.

What is worse is the negative interpretations the female raises concerning the above situation. She thinks her male is betraying her with another female and that he does not love her any more to the extent that hatred has started to penetrate his heart, or she no longer enjoys charming femininity that can attract or arouse him. Or, she might think she does not, any longer, occupies the top of his interests.

All these facts will soon be converted into depression, anger, a desire to react against the male and extreme objection against his carelessness.

We should always remember that oxytocin is produced in the female's body in all emotional states; whether in the state of love or touch. In times of relaxation, rubbing or massage produces significant amounts of oxytocin in her body. In addition, oxytocin is produced when she breastfeeds her baby because this brings her closer to the new creature who came to fill her life. If the hormone of masculinity arouses energy, then this significant hormone – in her body – urges her relax and causes decrease of blood pressure. It also produces cholesterol reducers. This gradually makes the female go through a state of calm and tranquility. Nonetheless, this sometimes makes her feel afraid.

Oxytocin is also produced in the male's body. Nevertheless, what incites more oxytocin efficiency in the female's body is the hormone of femininity, i.e. estrogen which improves oxytocin function and has a different mechanism for the interaction between testosterone and oxytocin in the male's body. While testosterone functions in a dissimilar way to what oxytocin produces, estrogen and testosterone interact positively, in a completely different way to the testosterone and oxytocin interaction.

You have to bear in mind that production of oxytocin in the male's body negatively affects production of testosterone. This means when the male enjoys relaxation through massage done by his female, testosterone decreases in his body. However, massage and any other stimulus of oxytocin in the female's body interact positively with estrogen and arouse her desire and her emotional and sexual interaction with the male. Isn't it surprising?!

The woman who suffers from hormonal malfunction produces really big amounts of testosterone - which is contrary to the nature of her body or does not get along with the general acceptance average among females, especially the aggressive ones affects oxytocin in her body intensely and negatively. Therefore we find that the female whose body produces testosterone is always prone to nervousness, agitation and outburst at any moment. This very situation afflicts a female when she nears the menstruation where she experiences a sharp decrease of estrogen and a relative increase of testosterone. At this period of time, testosterone level become actually higher than estrogen, hence, the female will not be able to enjoy a positive temper; rather, she will be edgy and on the verge of agitation and outburst. In fact, a female is not very often positive at such a time.

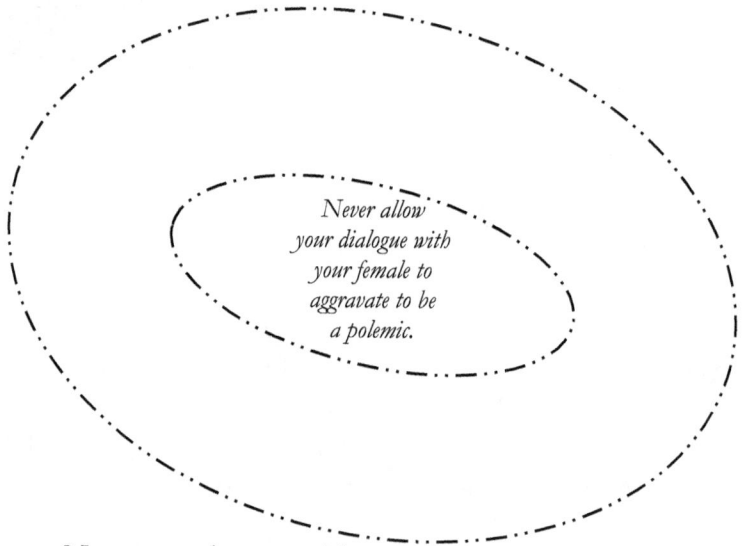

Never allow your dialogue with your female to aggravate to be a polemic.

No matter how positive testosterone in the male's body is, it might soon turn a male into a state of aggressiveness. Likewise, if testosterone increases a little in a female's body, it arouses her sexual desire; however, if it rises a lot, it will negatively interact with oxytocin. Consequently, this affects the nature and performance of the female and both; the male and female, will get into a vicious circle again.

Positive communication
between male and female

⬇

| Higher testosterone levels in male's body | Higher oxytocin levels in female's body |

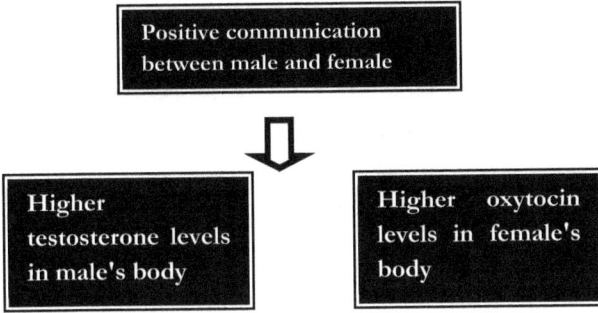

The couple has to go together on vacation so as to escape work pressure. If they cannot, they can resort to fun, laughter, joking and positive activities such as: doing sports or watching comedy movies. They can also do some daily participational activities like playing cards, or they can visit friends (together or individually) for a couple of hours. This, beyond doubt, helps them get into a state of longing and wanting one another.

The problem in the hormonal equation - between the male and female - lies in the fact that the testosterone levels in the male's body have to be high so as to start to care for the female. The female, on the other hand, needs the oxytocin stimulation as to return the male's care times doubled.

It is strange enough to know that a stressed male tends to make love so as to lessen his tension which is accompanied by adrenaline, cholesterol and testosterone. In fact, he needs a sexual discharge to attain balance.

The female, on the other hand, cannot make love unless the oxytocin rate is high. In other words, she needs to feel she is a female and to be exposed to care and sexual arousal in order to practice love.

There is a type of women who can have sex even when they are stressed. These are the nymphomaniac women who I elaborated on in my book "How a Female Thinks". This type of women has a high rate of testosterone. So, unlike the feminine nature, i.e., having sex only when oxytocin rate is high, the high rate of testosterone stimulates the female towards having sex. This comes under pressure and tension which accompany the high testosterone rates. However, those females can enjoy great peace and comfort, contrary to their nature.

We have to bear in mind the fact that the orgasm raises oxytocin, but it, temporarily, reduces the testosterone levels in the male's body. Therefore, a female would enjoy a temporary leave from desire, and she would rest after reaching the climax. BUT, her desire will not come to an end like the male. Nonetheless, there is a type of women who feel that whenever they reach the orgasm, they need more sex due to the high rates of testosterone in their bodies which rouse more desire and, consequently, more oxytocin which in turn reduces testosterone. Indeed, it is a highly complicated equation of interaction. This type of women, however, needs a special care and a special untraditional way of dealing.

As for the male, whenever he reaches his climax, testosterone levels decrease and his body releases oxytocin; a case that urges him to go to sleep soon after the elapse of this moment of intimacy. This situation affects the female almost negatively because after reaching the orgasm, she feels she is more in need for her male who hastens to fly away seeking rest.

This means that the male has to know his female's sexual nature. He should not make love with her unless she is nymphomaniac or one who demands having sex any time, even in times of pressure.

* * * * *

Who Can Do What

Women have a better memory than men with regard to the word they hear. The importance of this fact appears clearly through their heated arguments.

Rates of blood flow increase in certain places of cerebrum. Such places include those controlling language. This is one of the reasons researchers show as a conclusive proof of women having better capability of immediate recalling as well as instant and long distance recollection of the transmitted word.

Try to find contemporary solutions for a chronic problem with giving a sincere promise to find more durable solutions.

Among other reasons that prove the sharpness of woman's memory is her higher rates of concentrated estrogen. Men also have estrogen but in small amounts.

Testosterone is an important element in the formation of estrogen. There is an enzyme called "aromatase" that changes testosterone into estrogen inside the cells. Paradoxwise, the highest rate of estrogen is found in the protoplasmic cell of the cerebrum of a male fetus, and is responsible for giving masculine qualities to his cerebrum.

There is evidence that estrogen activates many neurons, increases blood flow to certain areas in the cerebrum and builds up complicated links between neurons. Moreover, high levels of estrogen are associated with the improvement of learning skills and memory. It could be the reason why women excel at such tasks.

It should be noted that estrogen is a key element in the recently discovered fact that says: "Women better recall painful events than men."

It is worth mentioning here that women find it easy to communicate verbally. They have richness and abundance in using words and expressions. Most studies show that women outmatch men at using language, in addition to their ability to speak easily and fluently. Compared to men, women not only use more words but also more diverse words and more accurate and meaningful facial expressions.

As far as seeing is concerned, males are better at seeing at a distance and estimating depths whereas females are better at side vision. Males can see better in bright light whereas females are more efficient at seeing at night. Females are also more sensitive towards ranges of the red colour than males. They also enjoy a better visual memory and better perception of the meaning of facial expressions and context, let alone that they show mor capability at recognizing faces and remembering names.

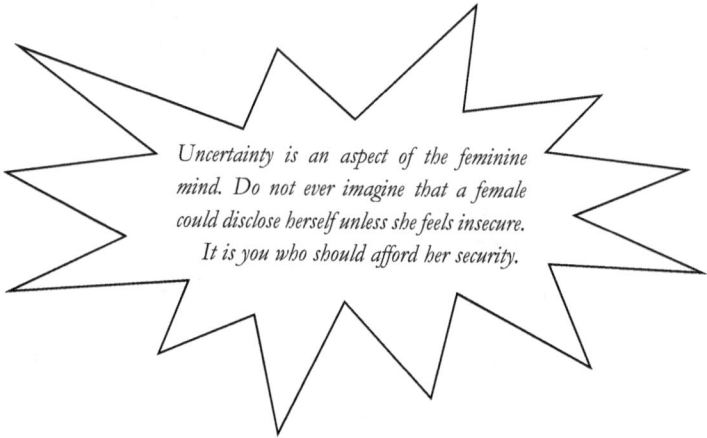

Uncertainty is an aspect of the feminine mind. Do not ever imagine that a female could disclose herself unless she feels insecure. It is you who should afford her security.

The centre of the ability to estimate places reveals seriou differences between males and females. The ability of estimating distances is located in the frontal right part of the cerebrum, bu this centre is not well- recognized in the case of women.

Professor Ruben Gur, a neurophysiologist from the USA Pennsylvania, has proved that the electric currents in men's brains decrease to 70% in the state of relaxation, and 90% in the case of women experiencing the same state. This is because women receive information from the environment and analyze it continuously.

One of the major reasons for the abovementioned is that there are 130 million needle-like cells called "vision receptors", and 7 million pin-like cells. However, females' eyes are different from males' eyes. Women can see in a more obtuse angle than men. The more the eyes receive   estrogen during the formulation of the eye while being an embryo, the wider the peripheral vision becomes. That is why the female cannot deal with spatial dimensions in the same way a male does, but she can see everything as regards details or things she is indirectly looking at. So, the eye and brain nature which were formed when she was an embryo makes her relation with space completely different from that of the male.

Do not hurt her feelings or offend her femininity. She will rapidly turn to her animus (the masculine spirit) to defend her anima (the feminine spirit).

In other words, women cannot deal with spatial dimensions the same way men can, but they can see the very details of everything or things that are not in the exact direction of sight. The eye and the embryonic nature of the cerebrum make the relationship with place a completely different one.

There is strong evidence that men and women deal with issues related to place in different ways. For instance, Dr. Maraianne Legato says that they have examined the way by which men and women can find their way accurately through an experiment conducted in Canada. They used a real labyrinth. Men and women not only activated completely diffident parts of the brain to deal with problems of place, but they used different strategies to find a way out. Women made use of the outstanding features of the place to know the right way while men used "the Euclidean information"; i.e., trying to imagine their places inside the design to get out of it.

Researchers found out that if any of the two sexes followed the strategies of the other to find their way out, both of them would do that inefficiently. Researchers concluded that there were real differences between the two sexes when it came to dealing with spatial issues.

It is important to note that both men and women activate a section from the right part of the cerebrum. Men also get the aid of a section from the left part of the cerebrum to solve spatial problems whereas women do not. For example, unlike women, men have a better ability to imagine the shape of a thing in a two or three-dimensional space.

Karren Christian and Rainer Kinsman; professors at Hamburg University, Germany, said that the high levels of testosterone in men were related to their excellence at spatial problems. However, those levels were related to their low ability in verbal expression which women excelled at.

> *When you hear a phrase like "You cannot understand me ", you will be committing a mistake if you think you are required to understand her ideas in a logical and successive way. She simply means that "you are not capable of realizing what my needs are.*

According to Alan and Barbra Pease, there is true evidence that the place-analysis ability inside the brain since birth results from a peculiar hormone for both sexes that is secreted during growing up. Little girls who have excessive secretion of the suprarenal gland suffer from high levels of male hormones. Those girls look manlike, even when born to the extent that their genitals are mistakenly thought to be male's genitals. They prefer tough games and they are possibly sexually attracted to women more than those who do not have this disorder. They also have a better ability to deal with spatial problems.

The evidence is better clarified by studies of Alan and Barbra Pease in an appreciated way. It also meets our vision and analysis of the mechanism of the activity of the two hemispheres of the cerebrum. It was proved that in the case of boy-girl twins, the girl benefited from the extra dose of testosterone from her brother. For instance, she had a high ability to imagine the three dimensions when compared to her non-twin sisters. That could explain her notable use of the left part of the cerebrum. She and girls of the like were sometimes seen driving in a way similar to the way of men as far as spatial recognition was concerned.

Alan and Barbra Pease say that Dr. Camilla Benbtow; a professor of psychology in Urea University, USA, scanned images for the brain of more than a million boy and girl so as to study the mechanism of spatial visualization. She discovered that differences between sexes were very clear starting from the age of four. Girls could understand the two dimensional pictures in an excellent way, while boys could do that in addition to recognizing the third dimension or the depth. Using video, the test showed that boys outmatched girls four times. It was not surprising that the worst boys excelled the best girls. This characteristic is located in many places in the brain. It is located in four places at least, in the frontal side of the right part. Women do not have special locations for this characteristic, so they have fewer skills in this regard. That is why they do not like jobs that need this skill and they do not have hobbies related to place image, unlike men who choose jobs and sports where the place skill is a must.

> *Beware assassinating the other with your words or anti-feelings.*

The right hemispheres of boys' cerebrums grow more rapidly than the left ones. The neurological connections in the right parts are ready before those going to the left parts and they are bigger in number. Girls' cerebral hemispheres, on the other hand, grow at the same rates. That is why they have more skills than boys. They have more neurological connections between the two hemispheres. This means that the corpus callosum is thicker. Because of this, we find more right and left-handed girls at the same time than boys, but those girls have a difficulty in distinguishing between the two hands instantly. Testosterone hampers the growth of the left part of males' cerebrum, but it helps the right part grow in a faster and better way. This makes the ability of comprehending space develop strongly.

Studies conducted on boys and girls between five and eighteen showed that the boys were much more able to hit a target or to point to a beam of light and to redraw an ornament depending on memory as if they followed the lines they had in their imagination. They also had a better ability to join separate parts in three-dimensional groups and to solve math problems. All those skills, in 80% of males, were located in the right hemisphere of the cerebrum, according to the studies.

The American scientist Dr. D. Wechsler developed a group of IQ (intelligence quotient) tests in which he avoided fields where excellence was related to sex. The study was conducted on people from different levels of education, including primitive societies. He could reach the same result reached by some other independent researchers. Dr. D. Wechsler said that the IQ of women was 3% higher than men despite the fact that women's brains were a bit smaller. But, when labyrinth was the test, men, regardless of their education, got 92% of the correct answers; women got the remaining 8%.

> *When a woman advises you, this does not mean she does not trust you or she is constantly trying to have control over you. She plainly wants to share and communicate.*

Know Your Partner's Representative System ... Deal Accordingly

If you want to know how to deal with a partner, you ought to discover their system first. A person may be visual, auditory, olfactory or kinesthetic. There are special characteristics and attributes of each type.

A visual person speaks fast and loudly and breathes quickly. They are always active and energetic and their decisions are based on what they personally see or visualize. Thus, their use of language would be specific. They use photographic language such as: "I am in the picture now" or "Let us envision the whole issue". They use utterances like: "I see"," I notice", "clear", "imagine", "landscape", "shape"...etc. They, through their life experiences, show more interest in views and sceneries than in sounds or sensations. When they stand, they go a bit backward with their head and shoulders upward. And if they want to recall something from the memory, they look over their eye level.

You can also detect a person's modality through his/her eyes and expressions. Hence, when a visual person answers a question which answer is ready in their memory, their eyes will move upward then leftward to remember the piece of information required. When you ask them what colour their car is, their eyes will move upward then leftward.

However, when you ask them a question that requires some thinking, you will see their eyes moving upward then rightward to visualize the image. For instance, when you ask a visual person to

visualize a winged dog, they will form an image of it since this piec
of information does not exist in their memory.

A visual person talking to themselves; i.e., having an intern&
monologue, does not move their eyes at all. They may be lookin,
in your direction but not looking at you. They will be searching fo
an internal image (either by visualizing it or recalling it).

An auditory person uses different sound pitches in on
conversation. They breathe comfortably and they have great abilit
of communicating with others without interrupting them. The
show more interest in sounds than in sights and sensations of a1
experience or incident. Their decisions are made according to wha
they hear and according to their own analysis of the situation. The
say things as: "I listen to what you say", "these words sound
good" and "I hear". They also use such concepts as "rhythm"
"music", "silence", "accent", "sound"... etc. When they stand, the
lean a bit forward with their head rightward or leftward and thei
shoulders back. However, when they want to recall something, the
look straight ahead towards the horizon.

When you ask an auditory person who already has an answe
for your question, their eyes will move leftward then forward o1
the ear level, and then they remember the sound. Thus, when
asking an auditory girl to talk about her favorite song, her eyes sta
in the same level but they move leftward.

Upon asking an auditory person about something they do no
have a ready answer for, their eyes stay at the same level but mov
rightward to imagine and create new sounds. When you say to you1
auditory friend that their car sounds like barking, they will create
auditory images since this piece of information is not available i1
their memory. Their eyesight will stay at the same level but mov
rightward.

An auditory person talking to themselves will look downward then leftward. If your auditory friend wants to quit their job and are thinking of a way of doing that, their eyes will move downward then leftward.

A kinesthetic person, however, is usually quiet and speaks in a low voice. They breathe slowly and give more attention to feelings and sensations than sounds or images. Therefore, we notice that their decisions are sensation-based. Others can affect their sensations, consequently, their decisions. They stand with their head forward and shoulders downward. And when they use their imagination, they look down their neck. They use words and phrases such as: "We are about to catch the thread that will lead to solving the problem", things are moving smoothly", "I feel", "I touch", "I sense", "cold", "comfortable", "quiet", soft"...etc.

When you ask a kinesthetic person how they feel when they fall in love with a person, their eyes move downward, then rightward while they are trying to recall this sentiment.

It is worth mentioning that recalling is always on the left side and visualization on the right one.

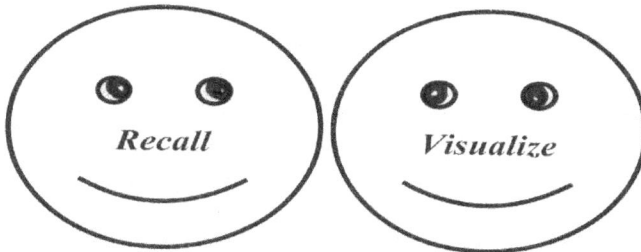

Having noticed the representative system of others and their linguistic evidence and eye gestures, you realize how they build information in their minds. Hence, you can communicate with them on the same level. This helps you become almost skillful in communicating and helping them solve their problems via hypnosis.

When we come to know that our partner is an auditory person, we realize that speaking is their distinctive means of communication. If they are visual, then seeing is a priority. Therefore, they have to be looked at especially if your partner is a female. The male's appearance has to be well-approved; i.e., he should not look repugnant. As for a kinesthetic person, touching their body every now and then triggers their sense of communication.

An olfactory person would like to be hugged, for hugging would make them feel connected. Hugging, then, is a way of communication since it helps an olfactory person communicate through their nose.

Olfactory people have their own chemical-like equations that should be noticed and taken into consideration. There is a reality that cannot be underestimated: "We get attracted to others through our sense of smell." Hence, different odours have a different impact on us.

Lavender helps us calm and to sleep while pine provides us with energy. But as regards human odours, recent experiments show that the odour of the husband's armpit may end his wife's tension (though this may not be attractive over time). Anyway, females are known that they have a better sense of smell than males, probably because of their high rates of Estrogen.

In fact, every person has their own distinctive odour which acts like a fingerprint. According to some recent studies, newborn babies can distinguish the males from females through their odour; a case that scientists call "odour type". Thus odours play an effective role in the life of those whom we get attracted to.

The abovementioned modalities are interrelated. A person may be all of them. This is determined by the type a person is as a *"situated knower"*, i.e. according to the formation of their cerebrum at the mitosis stage. We have to remember that one of the modes of communication with a person, especially a female, is *"smelling"* which can even be more important than any other sense. The sense of smell is often related to the kinesthetic type.

However, all types (visual, auditory, olfactory and kinesthetic) have something in common; they all need to compliment their appearance. To know how to deal with your partner, you can also know about their personality form the colour of clothes they like to wear because every colour has significant effects on people's psychology.

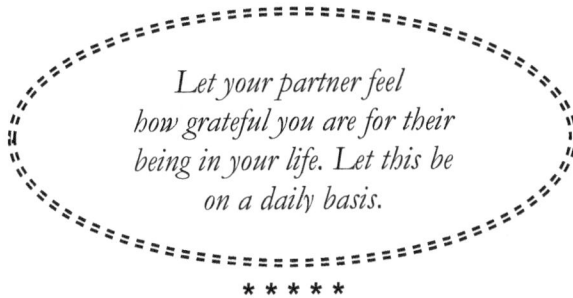

Let your partner feel how grateful you are for their being in your life. Let this be on a daily basis.

* * * * *

The Polemic State between Males and Females

No matter what difficulties we; males and females, face, they aggravate dramatically when we argue. During an argument, the amygdale; the part that controls emotions, is highly activated whereas the frontal cortex, which is the part of the brain responsible for rational thinking and problem solving, is less active at that time. This is the reason why it is difficult to maintain focus on targeted points or talk in a coherent manner. This also applies for women with previous unpleasant experiences similar to the current situation they are undergoing. Women's memories of those situations and arguments are clearer and more detailed in comparison to those of men.

When you are angry, your brain is in a state that is remarkably similar to that of an orgasm (the climax of sexual excitement). That is why people say things that they regret saying after a warm embrace. In both situations, our minds act against our own interests. To put it differently, our emotions at that point are exaggerated and the centre of logical thinking is stalled.

In a state of excessive fury, the brain releases more hormones into the blood stream. One of the differences between males and females is that these levels of hormones return to their normal proportions very slowly as far as females are concerned. While a male calms down quickly, a female finds it difficult to do so. This explains why the male mistakenly thinks the problem has come to an end only to find out that his female has returned to the fighting square with new creative reasons for arguing.

Researcher J. Carter believes that when a person is tense (whether the reason of this tension is psychological or organic, as in the case of injury or illness), the body secretes a number of hormones.

For instance, our bodies produce *"adrenaline"*; the attack-and-retreat hormone, that affects our perception, therefore we feel estranged from our surrounding circumstances. To us, everything seems to happen at a slow pace. At the same time, when blood pressure increases to the utmost level, we feel strong heartbeats within the chest followed by shallow and rapid breathing, and then our senses become sharper. This explains why when we are exposed to a distinctive smell or provoking colour, our brain displays a mental image of a previous experience that we had when we were very tense.

Our bodies also produce a hormone called *"cortisol"*, known to everyone by the name: *"tension hormone"*. One of the basic functions of cortisol is to regulate blood sugar.
When secreted at the times of tension, it stimulates the body to pump more energy into the blood stream. At the same time, it stimulates the cells to consume the minimal amount of it. This clearly indicates what important role the cortisol plays in regulating blood sugar rates in certain

cases, such as when you forget to eat which sometimes occurs when you are exposed to great pressure at work. It also explains why many people who undergo constant pressure suffer from overweight. The reason is that their bodies are constantly trying to harmonize their energy levels to fit the fluctuations of the blood sugar levels caused by cortisol.

Researcher J. Carter noticed that low rates of cortisol are very useful for the body since they help increase the body's efficiency in facing the danger of the tension causes. However, high rates of cortisol secreted when exposed to constant tension have a devastating effect on the cells of the immune system because the high rates hinder cells from effectively performing their functions, weaken the immune system in general and make our bodies more vulnerable to contagious diseases.

"Ohio State" University researchers have found out that th causes of tension such as approach of exam time can cause a dela in the healing process of the wounds that appear on the mouths o students. As for the women who undergo a relative suffering fror Alzheimer, they do not recover from an illness as quickly as wome of the same age and who have never gone through the sam experience.

The fact that we are more vulnerable to diseases when w shoulder a heavier burden than we can handle is not somethin illusionary because our exhausted immune system fails to take o the additional task of fighting a virus or contagious disease.

Tonsilla cerebelli controls the secretion of adrenaline, cortiso and all the other chemical elements released by the cerebrum unde the influence of tension. It is one of the old systems that exist ir the cerebrum, and that are necessary for our survival. It is a part o the cerebrum that consists of a cluster of nut-shaped cells locatec at the bottom of the cerebrum. It helps us in the process of storin emotionally-charged experiences in order to become part of th memory so that we can take a decision of escaping or defendin ourselves in a proper way when the same accident happens onc again.

The cornu anmonis; *"hippocampus"*, organizes a systen composed of a number of nerve cells, thus forming a closed circui that contains memories of an experience within our minds. Ir other words, the tonsilla cerebelli helps us perform a complex series of calculations that determine whether we feel frightened or not and what we should do in case of fear.

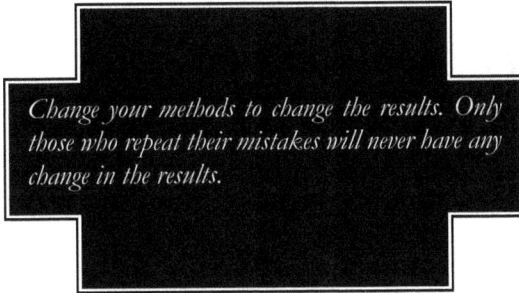

> *Change your methods to change the results. Only those who repeat their mistakes will never have any change in the results.*

Women's bodies produce higher levels of cortisol than men's bodies when subjected to tension which may last for long periods. Progesterone does not allow cortisol to stop carrying out tasks. Since cortisol helps to enhance the process of learning and memory formation, its high levels mean that women are not only affected very deeply by unpleasant events, but also remember them vividly. Contrarywise, the testosterone; hormone of masculinity, hinders the effect of cortisol.

Cortisol is a catalyst in the formation of unpleasant events memory. Tonsilla cerebelli is the other factor responsible for this formation because it is the centre that controls the feelings of fear.

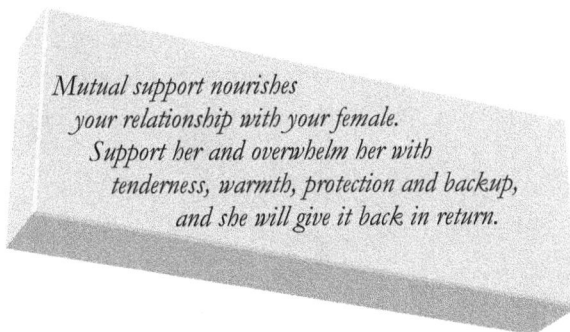

> *Mutual support nourishes your relationship with your female. Support her and overwhelm her with tenderness, warmth, protection and backup, and she will give it back in return.*

Researchers have come up with an interesting dissimilarity between the two sexes. During the formation of the emotionally charged memories, men use only the right section of their tonsilla cerebelli whereas women use the left section of it. Each of the two sexes uses different areas of the tonsilla cerebelli to affect the memory.

Women exercise the areas connected to other centres of the cerebrum such as the optical subthalamus and the brain stem. The brain

stem controls the respiratory system and the rate of heartbeat. Therefore, this regular movement in particular can explain why women are more responsive to emotionally charged memories. Men, on the other hand, exercise an area of the tonsilla cerebelli connected to recognition centres that are found in the upper parts of the cerebrum. This means that men can substantiate for more *"rational"* responses which depend on finding a solution to the challenge they face.

Despite the fact that women are the most vulnerable to tension which can lead to depression, they are far better than men when it comes to gaining back their psychological health after tension. This may be attributed to the fact that women are relatively stronger than men as far as enduring tension or anxiety is concerned because their frontal lobe contains a high percentage of gray matter in their cerebrum compared to men. This gives women an extra "cushion" or "pillow" of cells to protect them.

Moreover, estrogen functions as a neutral factor that reduces the harmful effect of a large number of tension causes on the nerve cells. That may help us know why illnesses such as schizophrenia begin to develop at a late stage of women's life compared to men, why women's response to low doses of antidepressant drugs is faster than men's, and why the side effects of these drugs are different. Perhaps this also explains why women retain most of their mental functions and capabilities with age.

> *When you suggest something to a female and she refuses, this means that she is – somewhat – willing … when she says "may be", this means she really wants it with all her heart. However, if she says "yes", be sure she is not a female because a female would never ever directly express what she wants.*

Women make use of completely different mechanisms to cope with tension. It is well known that men "isolate themselves from others" and, as a result, they suffer from a higher percentage of disorders that accompany tension like high blood pressure and addiction to alcohol or drugs. In contrast, women respond to tension by trying to communicate with others, especially with other women, hence, they make relationships through which they can talk about the problems they face and seek help. Such a response not only helps them cope with direct threats, but also protects them from the harmful effects of tension in general.

A recent research by Dr. Laura Cousin Klein and her colleague Dr. Shelly Taylor from the University of California, Los Angeles indicates that when tensed, women tend to eliminate their disputes, and initiate conversations with other women whereas men tend to isolate themselves from others. On the other hand, when men find themselves facing danger, they "inject" their nervous system with all the chemical compounds they need to engage in or escape from a battle (adrenaline, noradrenalin and cortisol). The result is that the pupils of their eyes widen, the rates of respiration increase and blood moves from the digestive system to the arms and legs in case they want to escape. Moreover, the speed of their reflex responses increases, but their sense of pain decreases.

Women share men all these responses, but they do not tend to use them. When a woman is subject to tension, the rates of oxytocin increase. This does not only help soothing her, but also motivating her to seek help which takes the form of starting a relationship with others, especially other women where she will have better opportunities in protecting her young child if she can

59

take care of him/her, or if she can get support and assistance in case of violent confrontations. Since it is well-known that testosterone resists the effect of oxytocin, we come to know why men and women have different responses when they encounter a danger or threat.

Woman
As Situated Sex and Psychology

Women and Depression

J. Carter mentions that a statistical study conducted in Britain showed that 7-12 % of men and 20-25 % of women suffer from pathologically diagnosed depression. A second study indicates that out of the nineteen million Americans suffering from depression, twelve million are women. Both Dr. Angst and Dr. Weismann, independently, say that the tendency of women to suffer from depression us a real thing and has a biological basis. Women are also subject to experiencing depression in a totally different manner; they feel depressed at a young age, suffer from tension and complain of many physical symptoms such as exhaustion, loss of appetite and sleep disorders.

Depression Drives

According to the biological, unilateral and reductive method of G. Carter, there is evidence that depression can be attributed to genetic factors. Dr. Casby and his colleagues at "King" University, London publicized the discovery they arrived at. The discovery shows there is a certain gene that has two different forms; "long" and "short". Persons who hold the short form are the most susceptible to depression. Dr. George. S. Zubenko and his colleagues from the University of Pittsburgh, Pennsylvania note that there are at least nine locations within our chromosomes that affect our susceptibility to depression. Many of them are related to the likelihood of women to have depression more than men.

The genes responsible for granting us our distinctive se control the release of hormones that continue to give us the sexua characteristics of the sex we belong to throughout our live whether we are males or females. For example, chromosome "y that exists only in males, "orders" the body to form the testicle which in turn produce the testosterone and the other masculin hormones, then the fetus changes into a small boy.

Fluctuation of the rates of hormones may be the key to fin out the reasons behind the widespread depression cases that inflic on women compared to men. There are convincing evidences tha link depression to the hormone rate fluctuation. When we observ women at certain times of their life, we notice that they are mor susceptible to depression shortly before menstruation and afte giving birth.

Because the fluctuation of hormone levels is a special natur of females, depression is common among females unlike male whose hormone levels are semi-stable in most times of their lives.

Pre-Menstrual Syndrome

J. Carter notes that one outcome of this monthly periodi continual pattern (the menstruation) is the occurrence of pre menstrual syndrome. Shortly before menstruation, the estroge concentration is at its lowest levels, and the levels of serotonin* ir the cerebrum are also low. It should be noted that the low levels of both estrogen and serotonin are related to depression.

Many women (almost 75%) suffer from a number of undesired psychological, physiological and behavioral symptoms in the days preceding menstruation.

---

* . Serorotnin is one neuro-conductor that helps stabilize the mood.

Severe symptoms that affect a small percentage of women (ranging between 2% - 8%) are classified by the psychiatrists' reference: *"Diagnostic and Statistical Manual of Mental Disorder"*, 4th edition, as having a real psychological disorder called Premenstrual Dysphoric Disorder or (PMDD). Women who suffer from (PMDD) are more likely to suffer from depression throughout their lives and are even more vulnerable to the risk of post-natal depression.

Many women especially those who are expectant mothers might get surprised of the emotional setbacks they undergo during pregnancy. Hormones certainly play a significant role in the depression that accompanies pregnancy. The first and the last three months of pregnancy are the periods in which women are more vulnerable to depression and are also the periods in which the hormone levels become unstable.

In the first three months of pregnancy, we notice some symptoms that include: sleep disorders, loss of appetite, mood swings, excessive sense of fatigue, and frigidity in addition to anxiety over the changes that will take place in a woman's life. All these things may play a role in increasing the sense of anxiety and depression. In the last three months of pregnancy, many women begin to feel seriously worried of the long-awaited birth process and of the difficulties that accompany it.

Natal Depression

J. Carter states that extreme changes of the hormone levels occur at this particular time; i.e., after birth. In the first week after birth, the estrogen levels reduce severely. Since estrogen is the hormone responsible for organizing the tasks of the neuro-conductors in the cerebrum, it may cause a sudden drop in the accomplishment of this task that is responsible for the psychological state control.

In severe cases of post-natal depression, the mother that has recently given birth to a child may suffer from psychosis and is twenty times more at risk of undergoing depression in the first month after giving birth than at any other time of her life.

Menopause

At this stage of a woman's life, hormones also play an active role. During the period preceding the actual cease of the menstruation, a woman is subject to periods of sharp rise and fall in the levels of hormones which make the regular ovulation process become unstable or irregular. This increases the levels of estrogen and progesterone. In other months, the pituitary gland secretes the ovulation stimulant hormone several times, however, this does not lead to ovulation and the hormones levels drop once again.

> *Do not look for supremacy. Look for participation.*

Since estrogen closely relates to the efficiency of the cerebrum in performing its functions, any decrease in its levels will surely lead to a serious effect. During menopause, some female patients' thinking ability weakens evidently. One of them calls that *"the perplexed mind"*. They are so perplexed to the extent that they are convinced they are on their way to lose their minds. They wonder whether it is necessary to have a medical checkup to be reassured that they are not affected by Alzheimer. In this period, they may lose their car keys, glasses or any other thing that does not belong to them and it seems they are not likely to remember names of places or people they have known all their life.

Genes and hormones cause a real difference in the chemistry of the cerebrum of both males and females. They can play an important role in woman's vulnerability to depression. For example, the bodies of men produce serotonin which induces optimism 52% more than women and their blood contains higher levels of serotonin compared to women. This may at least be part of the reason why women get more depressed than men.

Feminine Jealousy

Jealousy is certainly a subjective act which one projects on him/her self. In fact, it is an act that interrelates to one's self-estimation or self-image that is preserved in the consciousness and subconscious of both males and females. Jealousy is peculiarly a feminine privilege. It relates to the identity of the female who considers herself as the optimum value of existence and the most important being on earth since she is Eve (Elle). Therefore, she is never lenient when it comes to her identity.

In this respect, a female says:
"For me, jealousy is the most painful feeling not because I am different from others, but because it seethes none but me. This issue is very critical because I tend to classify jealousy into different categories, yet they all fall under jealousy. I often classify jealousy into positive and negative in order to pacify its impact on me. Nevertheless, I believe I actually deceive myself by such classification since jealousy is nothing else but jealousy. "Whenever I am emotionally attracted to someone, my selfishness erupts. I will, indirectly, strive to become the centre of his attention and to take over his mind so as to guarantee that he is mine; only mine, and no one else will share him with me."

Unlike jealousy of the masochist female who enjoys her jealousy as a means of self- torture, jealousy, from a psychological point of view, is a representation of an inferiority complex and intense self-disparagement. She expresses that either by silence which will consequently end up with self-decay and self-consumption, or by emotional outrage up to the point of physical violence like breaking dishes, throwing food or self-injury. The aim behind such acts is to vociferously draw the attention to her excessive suffering. Furthermore, some females would resort to verbal violence like lashing insults and undermining their selves or the partner's self with demeaning words. In such a situation, the female claims she is unable of controlling herself. This is only partly true but still it is inaccurate. It is true that she outbursts emotionally but she deliberately exaggerates these emotions in order to show how great her suffering is. She makes others part of this suffering by extremely hurting them.

Jealousy has a touch of narcissism. Thus, a jealous person has a narcissistic wound. In the case of the female, her own self has transformed from the state of a "master" to that of a "slave", so she combines the ambivalence of *master-slave*. And because her narcissism has been badly affected, she has no concerns ever for the feelings of others at the moment of her jealousy outburst.

To understand the narcissistic aspect of jealousy, we would present it as follows:

Narcissism

"Narcissism" means *"self-love"*. The word originates from Narcissus; the well-known flower. It also has roots in Greek mythology which tells about a nymph named *"Echo"* who fell in love with young Narcissus and became ill out of her love to him until she withered and died. Her death irritated the Goddess Nemesis, so she punished him by making him fall in love with his

own reflection on water. He became totally obsessed with his reflection until he was mentally and psychologically worn out. Then, one day he went into the water to embrace his reflection and got drowned. On the spot of his death, a narcissus flower grew and kept appearing each spring on the water .

A narcissist is someone who is emotionally immature. When we are young, we begin with loving ourselves, however, as we grow older, we start to love others and have objective interests other than our own subjective needs and pleasures. But, an immature individual is the one who is psychologically fixated at the primary phase of childhood. His/her activity remains restricted to themselves and consequently their cognitive horizon narrows and that makes them subject to failure and inadequacy. In order to avert such feelings, they disclaim any responsibility, live for themselves and exaggerate their self-estimation so as to compensate their feeling of inadequacy since they are inexperienced and self-centered.

"Narcissism" is different from *"egoism"*. Egoism is the estimation of people and objects with regard to the value, importance and interest they serve an egocentric person whereas narcissism is self-love. It is even referred to as self-adoration. It should be noted that the sexual element is frequently one of the meanings of narcissism. Krafft Ebing, for example, reports that some patients are not able of masturbating unless they look at themselves in the mirror.

"Narcissism", however, is different from *"egotism"* in that the latter is a form of excessive self-estimation and admiration to the extent of bragging and pretentiousness, as it is the case with schizophrenic patients who deify themselves. To put it differently, such people are in love with themselves to the point of idolizing themselves, surrounding their words and deeds with an aura of sacredness and rejecting any kind of criticism or discussion. This is the very meaning of *"egotheism"* or *"self-idolization"*. All of the

aforementioned can be embodied in what is called a *"narcissist character"*.

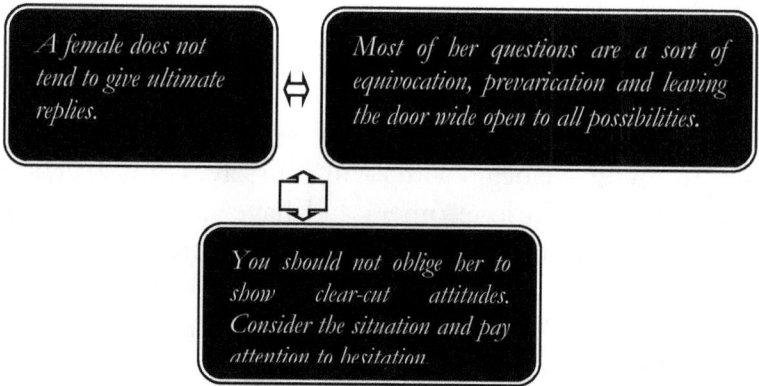

A female does not tend to give ultimate replies.	⇔	Most of her questions are a sort of equivocation, prevarication and leaving the door wide open to all possibilities.

⇩

You should not oblige her to show clear-cut attitudes. Consider the situation and pay attention to hesitation.

Narcissists are very much in love with their selves and are extremely self-assured. They are unconsciously deluded by their self-value and superiority. They consider it their right to obtain privileges and to get yet not give. Their philosophy in life is based on the presumption that their desire of something is their justified means to posses it. Moreover, they believe that people are no more than a means that will let them reach their longed-for ends. The narcissist female behaves with all the members of her family as if she were their master. She wants them to be exactly the same as any object she possesses.

In making sex, such a female only takes but doesn't give. She demands her own pleasure but not the pleasure of her partner thus, rarely does the partner reach his orgasm. Her sexual intercourse with her partner is infrequent because she barely allows herself to reach orgasm. If she desires him, she fulfills her desires regardless of his. Their sexual intercourse lasts to as long as *she* wants. However, if she tries to let him reach orgasm, it will be only because she wants to prove her sexual superiority and to keep hold of him as part of her own property. Moreover, she only chooses a handsome partner and tries to make him the most elegant man of all because she intends to boast about him. In most cases, narcissists do not enjoy successful marriages.

Narcissists also suffer from what is called a narcissistic self-observation; she enjoys exposing her nakedness in public as well as opposite a mirror. In other words, she loves her nakedness to be observed by her and by others. However, this tendency of self-exposition grows within her and later becomes an inclination to observe other's nakedness.

Psychological blindness is the foremost characteristic of the jealous female regardless of how high her education is. When it comes to those whom a female is in love with, she acts like any of those who are mentally retarded.

A female says that jealousy is her trait. She adds: "When I feel jealous, I never think; all my senses paralyze, any logical thinking just blurs and fades away, and then I am no longer able of understanding or comprehending anything. Nothing concerns me as the moment when my partner is with another woman. I find myself fancying him telling her whatever he would tell me and do with her whatever he would do with me."

Going through the previous words, we come to realize that this woman confirms the actual paralysis of any logical thinking whatsoever. This can be attributed to the fact that when a female of a narcissistic character is provoked by jealousy, her testosterone level increases. That actually explains her hostility. Testosterone, in turn, decreases her level of serotonin, thus causing dysfunction of the frontal lobe that controls, as we know, the process of sound judgments. That is why a jealous female loses her wisdom.

A jealous female is an alienating being for both herself and others. She is psychologically blind and she drives her partner to loathe her. She is psychologically immature and she does not have that self-understanding so as to acknowledge her responsibilities, duties or the rights of others. The most dangerous consequence of such a manner is her partner being reluctant and averse of her Clinics are the best indication of such cases since they have witnessed a variety of cases of men suffering from sexual impotence due to their partner's jealousy over them.

A jealous female cannot shoulder responsibility. Therefore, she adopts a mechanism of projection. She projects responsibility on others accusing them of torturing and distressing her because she does not respond to them or to their authority. She often figures out something that would make her look like she has been "victimized". The female, very often, holds the other person responsible of her hardships.

Discussion with a jealous female is *"mission impossible"*. The male, in this case in particular, should not be deluded by the fact that discussion is possible or even valuable. The frontal lobe, at this point, is deactivated and only the ego of the right cerebral hemisphere is now at work craving to dominate with the same dictatorial mechanism of the left hemisphere. Here lies the paradox. As the right cerebral hemisphere tries to apprehend, the neuroconductors of the left one exchange roles with it and urge it to behave in a way that contradict its function especially that the part controlling judgments in the frontal lobe is in a state of deactivation.

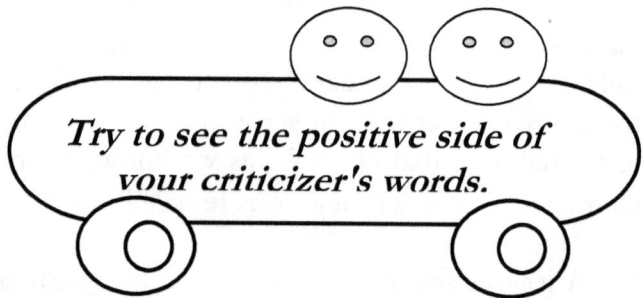

Try to see the positive side of your criticizer's words.

In the case of a jealous female, the reasons of jealousy are often illusionary. They are the result of the way she adopts in interpreting her partner's behavior in accordance to her own skeptical nature. The psychological path of a jealous female goes in one direction, for she always craves for more and more giving that has no limits whatsoever.

All desires of a jealous female should be fulfilled by having her partner ready to own her, and by binding him to a life that conforms to her own standards; the standards that would relieve her from jealousy. Thus, she would be asking him not to have any external life. This is, undoubtedly, impossible because she cannot but feel jealous. Moreover, as a narcissist, she would feel that she; only she, must be idolized. All attention has to be directed towards her and she must have all affection. However, if her demands are not met, she feels that her femininity is insulted and that the other person does not love her. This explains why a jealous female often says: "you do not love me, that is why I do not love you and I do not want you."

Mistrust and feeling threatened are two concomitant traits of the jealous female. She suspects all those around her, observes them carefully, and perceives their conduct as a tremendous danger as well as a genuine desire to plot conspiracies against her. Also, she does not trust any male; neither does she trust any female. She suffers from a pathological skepticism to the extent that even the slightest insignificant details would provoke her to an aggressive hostile attitude.

A jealous female suffers from two major fears in her life; the fear of competition and the possibility of losing her lover. Her narcissism is somewhat associated with *"the castration complex"* (metaphorically speaking) that arouses her fears over losing her lover.

Psychologically speaking, jealousy is a state of neurosis and a severe sense of inferiority often mixed with competition, envy, possessiveness and skepticism. *"Competition"* is a healthy positive state as long as its motivation is the accomplishment of a better situation and a distinguished position in life.

"Possessiveness" is similar to jealousy except for the existence of a third party. It is a state in which the female demands her partner's full attention and consideration, not out of fear of losing him but because she believes that her self would be insignificant without his love. Consequently, if such a female is to be left alone, she becomes overwhelmed with feelings of isolation and estrangement and she would even reflex to an infantile state.

Jealousy and possessiveness crisscross at the excessive need to be loved and appreciated. Nonetheless, possessiveness comes out to surface when the female feels valuable and that happens only when she is loved by her partner. However, in the case of *"envy"*, there is a tendency to defeat the other woman as long as she has whatever the envious woman does not. Envy is an extremely aggressive, negative and defeating feeling whereas skepticism involves *"scrupulosity"*.

Females and Pregnancy

Contrary to the fact that pregnancy is a feeling that is almost the same among people, its sensations are deep inside and are far from being coped with the details of or perceived by a man. Nothing will more clarify this than the words of a female in a letter about her first day of pregnancy even though she was firmly rejecting it at the beginning due to her desire to live freely:

"I didn't expect my first day. I never had the chance to imagine what it is like (to be pregnant) nor what it is going to be like after pregnancy. It would be more logical that my first day should be as normal as the day before and almost as any other day of the week. I am leading a seven-day life. Each day has a program that is being repeated almost identically week after the other. What happened was totally different. I could not but give up any routine ever since I saw the two pink lines in the middle of the home pregnancy test tube.

I laughed whole heartedly and I called my mother and husband with a voice playing a new note. I recalled all what I have read, heard and watched about the first day of pregnancy as I was tenderly rubbing my belly.

It was a sudden, unexpected and rather undesirable result. However, still joy grew inside me as it was tickling places that nothing could ever reach before. It was a deep joy…brand-new joy. It was fresh, nice and interestingly getting larger and larger.

> *Do not make your partner suffer from constant anxiety. The rule which says: "Live in danger" is not always suitable to harness ultimate and renewable energy.*

For two weeks or so, I have been suffering from a pain at the bottom of my back which I attributed to the extra work I have been doing lately. I had a very bad headache that couldn't be stopped by four Panadol tablets a day. Once I had to swallow two tablets of Setacodayine Extra to save myself the strong headache pains which I first ascribed to the approaching of the period, and I thought that staying up late and fatigue were the reasons for its delay along with my backache. I thought diet was behind my nausea though I didn't lose any one gram.

I did not expect at all, not even for a second, that pregnancy was the reason behind all this. I didn't know why I excluded such a reason this time in particular. I would not have thought that would be that happy to hear such news.

This embryo which is in my belly now... somewhere inside me....was not something or somebody I was waiting for. When think about it, I would feel I am on cloud nine out of motherly joy. Here lies a small mass of meat growing inside me and soon it will turn to be a fetus...a baby of my own. Would it mean anything to you if I say that being pregnant made me feel I am a perfect female and that my femininity has really become complete?!!!

That day - in the evening - I lay on my back in the clinic to confirm pregnancy after describing symptoms. My eyes were fully attached to the magical screen while the doctor's hands were brilliantly moving a device on the bottom of my belly.

You would not imagine my laugh when I saw that small mass on the lining of the uterus. My husband was asking me to calm down and the doctor was astounded by the fit of laugh I had. Two weeks ago I told my husband that I did not want to conceive a baby; it was not the suitable time then. Now, I am really afraid of the painkiller tablets that I have had a lot recently. However, the doctor assured me they would not harm my to-be-fetus.

So far, my embryo is four weeks old or more. I didn't expect myself to approve my conception with such happiness."

Such a text indicates a critical issue as far as females are concerned. It is the issue of the female's reaching full femininity by being pregnant. It is not a normal feeling
that moves from one generation to the other nor is it the result of social considerations.

The Changing Image of Motherhood

Andreas Bartels and Semir Zeki have found out that there are some real resemblances in the activities taking place in the cerebrum cerebration when we look at our lovers' photos. The round frontal cerebral cortex which is located just above the eyes becomes active when mothers look at the photos of their newborn babies. This part of brain is often known as *"the emotional brain"*. It is also responsible for recalling the preferable touches or the preferable smells and even the undesirable smells in addition to the face charm. The disorders occurring in this part of the brain are related to *"post-natal depression"*. The harm inflicting on the emotional brain may affect the natural sentimental connection between the mother and baby.

Perhaps the most important thing of all is the effect of the *"pleasure sensing centres"* when we look at our children's photos or when we look at people with whom we have a sentimental relationship. Feelings of love, whether for our life partners or for a four- year old child have a wonderful impact. In fact, the two sentiments provoke the same centres of pleasure-sensing which manifest themselves when we taste a piece of chocolate or get a financial reward at work. This explains why cocaine addicts find it so hard that they cannot quit it.

You cannot assume that all your thoughts are exceptional, necessary, current and exigent and need the other to execute them on the spur of the moment.

A contemporary woman says women nowadays can live without a husband since the latter's role as a breadwinner has decreased in the current societies. This is because women today have jobs which enable them to be economically independent and they have health and old age security. Moreover, man's sexual role can be compensated for, but, a woman cannot live without a child of her own. The woman who becomes thirty years old and does not get pregnant tends to be very aggressive and envious.

Another woman wanders: "How can a female reconcile her daily needs as a female and her passion for love, femininity and life especially if we take into consideration that her concept of continuity is not the same as that of the man who achieves it through breeding? A woman does not seek to preserve her kind. Her behaviour and motives clearly show that she only seeks sentiment or the fulfillment of a sentiment she creates by herself through having a baby. She will be connected to that baby through a mutual relationship of a special nature. In this relationship, the woman practices creation and containment in the way that best represents her physiological structure. If she ever has a sense of continuity through containment, it would be a continuation of her self-centered narcissism. She depicts herself in her baby, then in her child".

Some researchers tend to say that a mother's love to her child is no more than a continuation of her selfishness or self-love. Those researchers stress, along with Edward Hartmann, that a mother's love to her child is a way of preserving her kind since there is no separation between her body and that of her baby. However, it is noticed that even before the baby is born, the mother sees it as a separate distinct entity. The evidence to this is the normal fears that a mother develops about the possibilities of miscarry. No matter what such a "physiological and biological union" between the mother and her fetus throughout the period of pregnancy is, nothing would justify the claims that motherhood is merely a means of preserving the kind.

During pregnancy, some mothers may have the feeling of an amazing magical mixing with their to-be-born babies as if their selves melted completely in their babies'. It is, certainly, a fake feeling caused by the integration of the organic processes which control the needs of both the

mother and her baby. This feeling is not enough when it comes to the fact that the two entities of the baby and mother have become one.

If narcissist mothers would often make *"motherhood"* a mere manifestation of *"self-adoration"*, still the proper motherhood is when a mother loves her baby for its own self not hers. Such motherhood involves considering the baby as an independent entity, not a satellite of the mother's entity.

Some psychologists claim that the sentiment of love (or the love relation) is just the opposite of motherhood (mother-baby relation) because love is unification of two separate persons whereas motherhood requires a separation of two persons who were already unified.

Motherhood often seems laborious for some women because it involves many conflicts; a conflict between self needs and preservation of the kind, a conflict between the mother's tendency towards maintaining union with her baby and the baby's aspiration of liberation and independence, and a conflict between the mother's narcissism and the necessity of sacrifice for the baby. Finally, it is a conflict between the woman's love of herself and love for her baby as a separate entity. That's why when a mother's love is proper, it oppresses the mere animalistic instinct and focuses on the baby who is considered to be an independent entity that tends to get out of the darkness of the organic life and gradually reaches the light of consciousness or feeling. Thereby, mother's love will be just like any other love as it sees the baby as an end to be reached "terminus ad quem" rather than "a starting point" or "terminus a quo"; i.e., what the instinct implies.

There are some theories that explain motherhood as "a mere affectionate mixing" between mothers, on the one hand, and the baby's organic needs, motives and desires, on the second hand. Supporters of this view tend to say that a mother is not present but through her awareness of the instinctive factors that control her relationship with her baby.

If we only take those factors into consideration, we would be committing a deadly mistake especially if we imagine that the actions a mother does while taking care of her children are the result of direct experience. Throughout this experience, the mother lives the biological needs and changing conditions of the baby according to the baby's expressions that she infers.

> *Think profoundly of your female's words and do not rush towards rejection. You might recognize, years later, that you have lost a lot which could have helped you progress if you have taken her advice into account. Scrutinize her proposals and thoughts, add the new and innovative ideas to your own list, then listen deeply to her and examine her ideas. Do not miss such a train because it is overloaded with innovative and precious objects.*

A similar adaptation can also be presented in the idea of ecstasy which a mother enjoys when she breastfeeds her baby and that of the baby when s/he is breastfed by the mother. This means there is a parallelism between breastfeeding and the baby's hunger. Such parallelism leads the mother to perceive her baby's hunger – in his/her consecutive phases - through direct intuition. Therefore, the mother is very often capable of diagnosing her baby's diseases in an intuitively lucky way that might astonish the baby's doctor. That is why mother's love is ever considered as a *"unique love"*. It is love that can never be compensated irrespective of the financial benefits. Giving birth to a child– as Scheller says – requires a separation of the mother and baby's bodies. But this separation - at least after birth – does not involve a complete rupture or a breakdown of the "prior-to-feeling" psychological and biological union.

This mother-baby union is still maintained without relying only on the mother's interpretation of the biological aspects through getting help of a set of *"physical signs"*.

Love is not a merely negative emotional state or purely affectionate affectedness. Rather, it is a positive and active state in which affection relates to activity. So, it is not surprising to find a mother who really loves and dedicates herself for her baby, and shoulders the full responsibility of sustaining and bringing him/her up.

It is not a coincidence that the word *"responsibility"* in Englis or *"resposibilite'"* in French is derived from the word *"response"* o *"response"* which means *"answer"* or *"response"*. This means that responsible person is the one who answers a question when aske and responds when needed or referred to because they have dee interest in what they love and because they know it is their duty t care for it.

In essence, motherhood is a psychological function assigne to a woman as she shoulders the responsibility for upbringing an taking care of the baby. Nevertheless, this is not enough. A mothe should not only protect and take care of her child; she should als provide her baby with all the reasons to love life and hold to it.

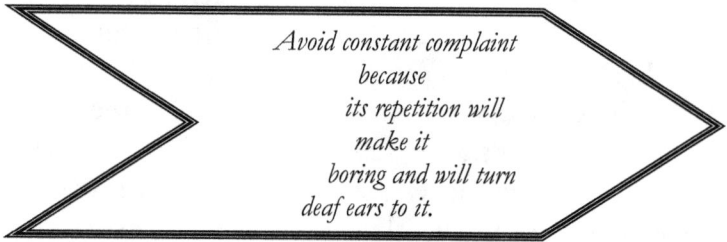

> *Avoid constant complaint*
> *because*
> *its repetition will*
> *make it*
> *boring and will turn*
> *deaf ears to it.*

The Torah has described *"the promised land"* as a *"land of mil and honey"*. We can similarly say that a real mother is the one who would provide her baby with milk and honey. By *"milk"* we mean protection and caring, while by *"honey"* we mean love of life an enjoying existence. Hence, if we are to precisely describe motherly love, we could say that it is an unconditioned love whic is based on giving rather than getting.

The word that denotes God's love to human beings and lov among human beings themselves in the holy books is *"rachamim"* which is derived from the word *"rechem"* that means *"womb"*. Thi indicates nothing but that the motherly love is the sublime exampl of love. Motherly love is unconditioned because it centres on th "existence" not the "behavior" of the baby, whereas the fatherl love is determined by some traits of the baby.

A mother would feel that the baby is *"HER BABY"*, and this is the first tendency that leads her to automatically cling to her baby even before its birth. That the baby is hers is a purely feminine feeling — something that a man would never have a match for. Therefore, a woman's tendency to give birth to children is essential and instinctive, but as for the man, it is a mere "desire" that needs to be justified or reasoned. It does not have the real tendency that a woman has.

As we mentioned earlier, the main feature that distinguishes the fatherly love from motherly love is that the first is restricted and conditional, while the second is unrestrained or unconditional. A mother loves her baby because it comes out of her belly — without fulfilling any conditions whatsoever. It seems that "unconditional love" satisfies a hidden need of human beings in general, not only of a baby. This is because each one of us wants themselves to be loved for their own self, not for any characteristic they might enjoy. This might be what Pascal meant by saying: "If somebody loves me for the traits or characteristics I enjoy, then they do not love me myself; rather, they love my traits".

When you feel that others love you out of admiration or because you could satisfy them, then you would feel, deeply in the inside, that you could not gain their love because you were only a means that would help them achieve their goals.

We all; children and adults, long for *"the unconditional love"* through which others would love us for "ourselves" not for "themselves". Although the majority of children enjoys such kind of love, many adults would face a difficulty in attaining it.

While the mother is likened to the nature, soil and land from which a baby comes out or in which s/he is brought up, the father does not represent any image of natural environment or habitat for the baby whatsoever.

The baby does not absorb or mingle father and mother into his/her super ego, as Freud suggests. Rather, the baby constructs two different consciences; one based on mother's law of love and the other on the father's law of reason and mind. It should be noted that the different psychological illnesses are no more than a manifestation of the adult's inability to strike a balance between the two consciences.

The baby is the mother's dearest creature ever because s/he is her own baby. Therefore, *"adopting a child"* may not fulfill the motherly needs of a woman since what is important for a narcissist is not the baby as much as the *"kindred"*. In fact, there is a big difference between the concepts of "baby" and "my baby" for such women.

Since the case is thus, we have to share Max Scheller his view in that motherhood is totally independent from woman's experience about babies because the sentiment of motherhood already exists in women who have never given birth and who might not have the least idea about it. Sometimes, they might not have any idea whatsoever about pregnancy itself. Hence, motherhood, as Helen Deutsch claims, is experienced by women who have never borne a baby and have never had a baby.

> *Avoid complete accuracy especially when dealing with feelings. Do not talk to her as if you were talking to a male. Do not discuss issues as if you were in a scientific seminar.*

We should admit that when a mother brings up her baby, she enlarges the circle of her existence and doubles the meaning of her life. Perhaps, one of the biggest secrets of motherhood is that the woman is given the chance to sacrifice her selfishness without losing her individuality.

The mother abandons her narcissism to gain a multiple personal life as she lives in the conscience of her children, but still she goes back to herself to enrich her life. It goes beyond doubt that when a mother responds to the call of real motherhood, she is then bringing her children up for "themselves" not for "herself".

> *When a female expresses her point of view emotionally, this does not mean that she adopts all what she declares. She is only thinking out loud.*

The changes that affect the female throughout pregnancy give an impression about the level of creation done by her in her wholeness. The following text expresses what a female says in her early days of pregnancy about delivering (innovating) a creature out of her.

"I look more beautiful with the additional kilograms that I have recently gained. My eyes are, like others' eyes, exhausted and they fully express what kind of life I am leading. The paradox lies in that this situation does not take away my happiness about my to-be-born baby or even my longing to hold it tight to my chest in my arms. I am totally distracted and pitiable!!

Perhaps, though I hate confession, the alternating hormones have beaten me. I am crying without a reason. This might seem to be romantic-like; however, the fact is that I am crying out of being touched. But, when I start, I cannot stop.

I feel sad because I have lost control. To stop crying, I try to define a cause for it. I have thousands of reasons not to cry (Note:

What is working here is the right cerebral hemisphere). I feel as if I were under the influence of magic or an anesthetic. Part of my consciousness is aware of what's happening to me (That is the left cerebral hemisphere), but it cannot help me find a way out or at least control a single detail (The right cerebral hemisphere).

I am not alienating myself from anybody, but I think I am not a useful friend to any one at this particular time. I am drowning more and more without a single solution to ease me or pick me out, and I am getting weaker at resisting circumstances. Problems are accumulating. I am no longer able of tackling them whether separately or as a full package. Problems at work as such have never occurred to me not even in dreams…My academic duties are very bad. Headache is always accompanied with nausea or the feeling of enfeeblement… let alone the lack of sleep that adds fuel to fire.

I wanted to cry and complain, but does anyone really need such a woman in his life? What am I crying for? …Nausea and vomitting… endless problems at work…more and more illusions. I am full of anger because my baby will receive a share of such negative feelings. I am so sad that I gave it this rotten dose, but I cannot stop it. I laugh at times and tell jokes joyfully at other times; however, one silly thing would get anger back to the peak. I cannot tackle issues alone… Am I disgusting enough? This text is highly significant if we want to access the internal world of the female during pregnancy. In short, for a female, pregnancy is a real cosmic experience.

Nasty Women

"Nasty women" cannot be regarded as a pure feminine phenomenon, for this entails the fact that there is another phenomenon called "nasty men". This is a pathological phenomenon as will be explained. However, some later syndromes could apply to men likewise.

A nasty woman is one who exercises control, punishment, or exploitation. However, a nastier woman is one whose conduct is immoral and who causes misery to people around her.

* * * * *

Types Of Nasty Women (As A Situated Psychology)

➢ The temperamental: A woman you can never expec which side of her character she will show in her persona relationships.

➢ The bully: A woman whose reaction cannot be predicted You will never be able to know when she will explode nor why sh is fuming in such a way. She will shake the whole sentimenta stability at home or at work.

➢ The ferocious: She follows the course of the bully woman but she feeds verbally and sentimentally on the victim tha constitutes a subject for her.

➢ The beneficial: A woman who establishes her relatior with the male on the basis of getting benefit. She does not do tha because she has the intention of harming others, but simply because her interest requires this act or that.

➢ The female living with the scum of society: She loiter; with unsuccessful people. She could be

wonderful with a nasty man but will not give such a chance to a polite man. She does not have enough self-satisfaction.

➢ The female living on the surface level with others: This woman loiters with people on the surface. She would abandon her husband and search for another from the surface if he begins to degrade and sink. She knows how to seize opportunities well. She would bluff even her dearest friends and take her husband to possess him for herself. Love and truth are merely meaningless words to her.

➤ The dependent: This woman holds to people she depends on and never abandons them. She cannot be an independent person.

➤ The masculine-like worker: She always abides by rules. She is not attractive and working under her supervision is not enjoyable. People had better meet her expectations or she will stealthily harbor deep hostility for them. She is never contended with anything and will not appreciate anybody whosoever. She does not use the word "encouragement" at any time.

Some women use these techniques because they have either experienced them or witnessed their mothers practicing them on their fathers. Some of these women are selfish and like deceiving and exploiting others for personal interests. Some of such women have no conscience, or only have the least of it.

This category of women enjoys some of the following characteristics. These women may:

- ❖ love to possess.
- ❖ be prevailing and may often have the penis-envy complex.
- ❖ be sentimentally unstable.
- ❖ have been misunderstood by others.
- ❖ be indifferent to others.
- ❖ be narcissistic.
- ❖ be self-dependant.
- ❖ be conscienceless.
- ❖ feel deeply within that she is better than others.

Maybe in the past these women were:

❖ sexually abused. This could have caused deformation and resulted in a self-regard complex.

❖ emotionally hurt, whether regularly or during critical situations of their life.

❖ sexually assaulted.

❖ neglected.

❖ exposed to shocks.

❖ badly brought up.

❖ accustomed to acting this way believing that it was appropriate to show their potential and responses.

Nagging: Situated Demanding

There is no doubt that criticism is essential to people's lives. It is a constant correction of shortages of anything in the universe. That is why compliant relations (in which one submits totally to the authority of the other) are incorrect. There is, however, a difference between criticism and nagging which goes even far beyond complaining.

The female's many remarks and comments on your faults do not necessarily target you personally. She assumes your perfection, and she wants you to be a god who fits her as a goddess.

Truly, some people cannot distinguish between criticism and offense. The language of criticism used by both males and females is often risky and is on the verge of giving the impression that it is the other that is targetted not their behavior or point of view. Normally, people do not differentiate between personality and ideas or behavior. Consequently, any criticism would be taken on a personal level by some people. We often notice that the person who undergoes criticism tends to be very defensive, and sometimes aggressive, defending their opinions and behavior as if defending their own selves. Moreover, they consider the one criticizing them as aiming to attack them personally and jeopardize their identity gradually. Soon, the criticized person counterattacks their critic to diminish them. Then, the two parties enter a non-stop cycle of criticism and counter criticism that would only aggravate small arguments into unsolvable ones.

A typical female does not generally exercise violent forms of criticism in romantic situations, for she will mostly be preoccupied with her right half (her emotions) which explains why the *"the loving soul cannot find fault,"* and why *"love is blind"*. However, nagging and complaining are among the typical characteristics attributed to the female without differentiating between this type of verbal performance and the concept of positive criticism that seeks reformation and perfection. Hence, nagging is the female's means of reminding the others that she, along with her feelings, needs to be the centre of attention in a way that would satisfy her ego as a female. This is neither faultfinding nor perfection seeking.

Interestingly enough, *"Nag"* is a feminine English noun that does not have a masculine equivalent. This means that there is a long-term accordance among most peoples to associate this noun with females. Moreover, British and American laws in the 19th century considered nagging as an act that requires punishment. The ugly punishment was to tie the nagging woman to a chair with movable arms and then drown her several times matching the times of her nagging and the number of her previous *"crimes"*. That was the famous procedure used in Britain and the United States to punish witches and prostitutes as well.

The aforementioned exaggerated punishment – certainly – did not take into consideration, according to the main stream of knowledge at that time and even at ours, how much injustice was bestowed upon the female by associating her constant complaining and endless nagging with crimes. They did not take into account her specific personal as well as biological aspects as a situated knower that had special private biological and psychological features.

The male tends to nag when the repetitiveness of discontent becomes the female's only way to subjugate him and make him go through a vicious circle of complaining. Hence, he gets out of control and logs into this "bad circle". The female believes that repetition will achieve a miracle that would make the other person respond to her feeling that she has all the right to express her annoyance of him. To this, he responds with more neglect. Eventually, this becomes a constant conflict where both parties are right; the female believes that the ultimate right lies in the male taking into consideration all the feelings and the small details related to these feelings. The male, on the other hand, considers this to be an intervention with his being, a violation of his uniqueness, and an illogical behavior against his individuality.

In fact, at this very moment, we come to see the most expressive contrast between the two hemispheres: the woman's right and man's left. They both identify with only one half; that is why they have two different languages.

The best evidence that they have two different languages lies in the fact that the right half of the cerebrum is programmed to do more than one task at the same time. This explains the many non-stopping issues raised by women, at a time when the man is completely lost listening to his woman talking and shifting from one subject to another, no matter whether she is tackling one violently repeated subject or several subjects at a time, or referring to something she fears in many different ways...

> *Emotion control is not a feminine characteristic. A female is fond of the man who never hesitates granting sentiment; however, she respects the one who controls his feelings and affords them when needed.*

This type of nagging aims at making the other feel guilty just as equally to the internal feeling of deprivation of something important. In other words, all that matters the right half as regards feeling, evaluation, intuition, beauty and communication may overshadow all that matters the left half; i.e., senses and logic.

The most serious aspect about nagging is that it goes on and on in a vicious circle and soon transforms from the circular motion into a spiral whirl dragging the woman to further anger, despair and rejection.

In most cases, complaining, and consequently nagging, does not occur for trivial reasons; it is a kind of demanding recognition of gratitude because the female, as a person who is constantly demanding communication, would always like to receive permanent approval and appreciation to recharge her giving ability and enhance her self-esteem especially if she feels that her life has become a mixture of trivial things that do not go along with her humane prestige.

> *Nakedness is part of the feminine entity. Female loves the game of nudity as long as she feels she is a universal container of love and sex.*

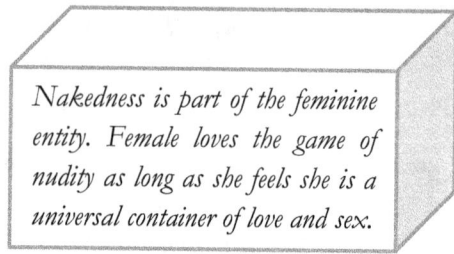

Though the female thrives to graciously give those around her, she believes that few words of appreciation or attention i something she really deserves, and is a way of recognition of the importance of what she dedicates herself to. The more he complaining is met with carelessness, the more her nagging will be This will result in seeking solitude, exploding (as a way of escape) getting frustrated or undergoing depression.

Complaining that leads to nagging is a proof of the interrupted communication between the male and female. Thus the only solution lies in all types of communication and the consideration of all the "hidden" requirements that arouse complaining. This needs exerting strenuous efforts on the part o men since they cannot guess what their females want and mean by their shower of words.

Very often, what the female focuses on through her words is not the real reason behind her outburst; it is her feeling o disconnection and all symbolic forms of emotional deprivation The solution a male could find might be simpler than just drowning into the female's ocean of words and issues. For example, offering his female a bunch of flowers, compliments, appreciation, and expressing how special and exceptional she is will be some simple solutions the male can resort to instead of wasting time going through details; and, as you know, the devil always lies in details.

The riskiest of all as far as complaining and then nagging, are concerned is that the parties involved become enemies in no time When a female nags, the male recalls the deep-rooted unconscious remarks of his mother. Hence, he would as if there were someone who wanted to get him back to the past and underestimate him as an adult. The result would be that he fiercely defends himself, thus, he loses connection and the situation aggravates. There will be a state of outrage and escalation. Hence, communication interrupts and eventually the two sides would more likely prefer to escape.

Here, we are not talking about pathologic personalities and "nasty" women. Rather, we are talking about the typical ones. This does not mean that pathologic personalities cannot be dealt with. The key to how to deal with the female, whether pathologic or healthy, is the same; attention and communication. Even masochist females find satisfaction in "negative" communication; what matters most for a female is to be profoundly understood and her demands fully realized.

Exaggeration

Since males utilize their left cerebral hemisphere more than the right one, which is the opposite case with females, the differences between both sexes in the degree of exaggeration stem from the fact that they are biologically different.

Once, my office manager burst into my office in tears. When I asked about the reason, she said: "I feel I would not pass my exams and would never graduate. As long as I failed two subjects, I will never succeed ... This is the first academic failure I have ever experienced in my life".

Analyzing such a situation, exploiting my left cerebral hemisphere and relying on my experience in psychology, I thought it was an exaggeration that resulted from lack of confidence, due to her home discipline that reposed on abashment, and her feeling that her female colleagues were more privileged than her as far as males are concerned. This was the result of a failing relationship that started with marriage and soon ended in divorce.

That analysis could possibly be accurate and precise if I were dealing with a male. But after I rested myself for a while to shake off the impacts of thrusting herself into my office, I began to think using my right cerebral hemisphere. So, I began to consult the feminine mind and the anima inside me which we; males, do not identify ourselves with, therefore, we lose every possible attempt to understand females. Even when we want to treat them, we utilize our masculine minds flagrantly.

There is no doubt that science depends entirely on the logic laid by masculine mind and that treatment should have a logical context. Nevertheless, understanding feminine cases should be based on the feminine mind.

Do not consider a female's anger as offending your manliness. Separate between the action and its background.

As soon as I began to think femininely; i.e., using my right cerebrum, I could realize that she; my office manager, was not suffering that much from an inferiority complex. She only wanted me to know how much worried she was. She wanted to indulge me in her psychological suffering which she reflected by resorting to the highest degree of emotional exaggeration. She wanted me to help her trust herself as much as she wanted to have emotional communication with her feelings and premonitions.

In that a case, I had to rely on my left cerebrum to have good analysis and to attain the details and way through my right cerebrum. Shortly, it was not, typically speaking, an inferiority complex. Rather, it was an emotional exaggeration.

WOMEN usually exaggerate when it is a matter of emotional estimation. They also make too much of things when it relates to intuition. However, when it comes to position and materialistic numeral issues, it will be **MEN** who tend to exaggerate.

Rarely does a female exaggerate over position or money unless she seeks to get a feedback that enhances her emotional side and feminine status. The same applies to males who do not tend to exaggerate but in cases of love or hatred, which are two feminine cases since it is the responsibility of the right cerebrum to deal with them. Males usually exaggerate over their job ranks, income, status, luxurious cars, achievements and the number of women they had relations with.

Such kind of emotional exaggeration appears clearly in those male and female artists, poets and actors. However, in cases of disconnection, we find that the female uses the highest degree of exaggeration to let her male realize how important her emotions are.

In an argument between a male and female on why she did not do the house chores, the female might say "I was busy". This sentence might be captured by the male who might directly ask about what was engaging her, then he would go back to what annoyed him at the beginning of the argument paying no attention to the exaggeration that she expressed in relation to her feelings. This is the very nature of the male's cerebrum which tackles the last word said then goes back to what irritated him in the first place through a flash back technique. One mechanism looks for materialistic details and the other resorts to emotional pyramiding. The male may start collecting evidence to logically confute his female while the female keeps her exaggeration going on. Thus, they will go into a vicious circle of exaggeration.

> *Things get value only when the male gets his female what she does not ask for; i.e., when he estimates what she is in need of.*

When a male exaggerates over his own characteristics, good deeds or status, other males view him as a liar and a silly person. However, when a female overstates her feelings, her female peers approve and blindly accept since it is a natural feminine act. What is remarkable is that when females meet males who overstate their traits (females' traits), they, get fascinated - at first - because they like fabulous appearances. But, they immediately and intuitionally get to know the reality behind this situation. Females contempt males of the like, nonetheless, they do not show the same contempt males show. They pass this over out of their own free will as openly and consciously.

Overstating affections and promises is part of the female's need which she resorts to when she feels she is neglected or emotionally depreciated. What matters to females most is "communication".

> *When a woman utters awful expressions against you, this means she is repeatedly assuring that you are unable of understanding her. She does not mean any harm. She is only using a language different from yours.*

Exaggerations are not a masculine mind preference since it deals with facts, figures and logical and literal interpretation of words. Therefore, males would deal on the basis of awareness that conforms to reality. All that does not match reality means it does not interest the male because it does not belong to the left cerebral hemisphere.

The language females use is a language of connectivity and friendliness, while language of males is that of social status, prominence and independence. So, we can say that cultural communication between males and females is a kind of communication between two opposing cultures.

If we are to translate the language of each sex into the other, we will not be in need of a "translation"; rather "compiling" which means the transition from an abstract language into a simple direct one, so to speak, as it is the case with computers where there is a transition from the analogous language to the digital one. This means both sexes speak two completely different languages.

According to some socio-psychological studies conducted on males and females, it has been discovered that job or self boasting is never a feminine characteristic; rather, a masculine one par excellence even if it pops up in some females. According to those studies, females do not boast their status (except for the esthetical feminine preference) nor do they give instructions. They set forth suggestions if they want to tell others what they prefer or like. They express that in a non-instructive language, i.e., a language of teamwork. They use such expressions as: "let us", "what about", "why don't we..." etc. However, when it comes to beauty, they sing a different tune. They might use expressions like: "I am better and more beautiful", "my beauty needs ...", "I deserve ...", "it suits me well that ...", "fancy: a female like me with such bad luck".

The way female uses to deal with others does not reach the point of exaggeration and direct opposition or challenge unless it touches her femininity. This especially happens when jealousy invades and overwhelms her. Recent studies conducted on males state that a male does not try to soothe conflicts nor does he keep harmonious social relations. Hence, exaggerating the role of the hero, leader, pillar or even Rasputin or Don Juan is nothing but masculine characteristic.

> *The female could express the feeling of fear through anger. You should differentiate between both of them. When she is at the prime of anger, slow down, and try to represent and realize the background of her anger. The fear cannot be removed unless its reasons are eliminated. The first step towards that is to feel she is protected.*

When a female falls ill, her emotional exaggeration gets more apparent. This is because she wants the other to feel how great her suffering is, on the one hand, and to enhance her feeling that her male is still in touch with her.

Both, males and females, need to use a proper language when dealing with the exaggerations of their partner; a language that entails positive and mutual understanding according to the following tips:

�֎ No party whosoever should say it openly that the other is exaggerating. The female should not show contempt for the male when he highly estimates himself or exaggerates over his uniqueness. The female should know that the need of the male to fulfill his virtual or exaggerated status (through understanding and absorbing) is the only way to sneak into him. She has to avail form this point and does not shatter it on the shore of reality since it is part of his masculine character and personal balance. The male, as well, should not decipher the codes of the female exaggerations literally. He has to view them as emotional expressions about something completely different; something he has to look for or, at least, early get and comprehend before he communicates it.

The way into a female's heart is by sympathizing with her and her emotions. Therefore, using expressions like the following ones is very important for a female: "I feel you", "I agree with you", "I sympathize with you", "I appreciate your emotions", "thank you for indulging me in what you feel", "you are much more important", "I will ever be with you and beside you" and the like.

The way into dealing with a male's exaggerations can be through the use of some phrases like: "you deserve more", "what you gained is only part of what you deserve", "I am sorry that it took me a long time to realize how important your ideas are", "thank you because you always do what makes me proud of you", "you are always great", "when I see your greatness, I feel I do exist"...

Receiving lovely words and feelings are a priority in her life on condition that she is not deceived. The feeling of being deceived will arouse a feeling of inferiority. This can only be avoided by joining words and actions.

Situated ... But ... Will Meet

Chemistry of Love among Human Beings

A research conducted by Dr. Donatella Marazziti, shows that the testosterone rates become almost the same for men and women when engaged in a love affair. Dr. Marazziti points out that although those people may go on in the same relationship, the testosterone rates return to their normal levels. This might explain the decline of the sentimental feeling of love among people after living it for a while; that is to say after living it as a normal life. Hence, our first love remains as vivid in our memories just because we have not experienced it before and because the first feeling it creates cannot be repeated but by another first love (in its early stages).

The first experience is accompanied, along with the aforementioned signs, with lack of the chemicals (dopamine, phenylethylamine, and noradrenalin) that characterize the period of getting infatuated with the partner. This period is also accompanied with an increase in some other chemicals that enhance the relationship and create the feeling of reassurance between the two partners.

Endorphin "The Magic Hormone"

According to Legato, Donatella Marazziti realized that after having a sexual intercourse, the endorphin which is also known as a natural painkiller, remains for a while. When engaged in a long love relationship, our brain produces the same chemicals that enable a marathon runner to get to the end line in the hardest circumstances. Endorphins enhance our feeling of happiness and affect profoundly our moods. Our bodies produce them at times of laughter too. This explains the laughter-based therapy and why females are more attracted to men who have a sense of humor. When rates of endorphin increase, we become sociable and friendly and we get a feeling of relaxation. This hormone is also produced at the peak of orgasm. Both, endorphin and oxytocin share the responsibility of giving a feeling of happiness after having a hot sexual relationship.

Oxytocin "The Cuddle and Romance Hormone

Oxytocin is a hormone that stimulates the sexual arousal among both males and females. The body produces larger amounts of this hormone during the sexual intercourse and after reaching the thrill. Oxytocin appears through a number of functions that do not apparently look related to each other. Historically speaking, the word *oxytocin* is derived from a Greek word means *"quick birth"*. It is related to muscle easy contraction at birth time and it stimulates the uncontrollable flow of milk for breastfeeding mothers. It should be noted that oxytocin is not only produced at times of happiness, but at times of tension, too.

The relationship among these different cases may be summed up by saying that all of them involve engagement facilitated by oxytocin. Researchers believe that the relation between the flow of milk and oxytocin strengthens the relationship between the mother and her baby. This might explain the low number of post partum depression cases among women who breastfeed their babies in comparison with those who do not.

> *Males overcome their nervousness when they have sex while females overcome it by being noticed, cared for and listened to.*

Like endorphin, the hormone of oxytocin leads to a better mood. That is why researchers call it *"the cuddle hormone"*. Negative ideas reduce this hormone levels in the body whereas some massage may help increase it. This is the reason why some people get addicted to massage and find it a way to love and have sex. Nevertheless, it is a way that leads to relaxation. It stimulates feelings of tenderness, kindness and communication. The secretion of oxytocin increases 20% during a massage session for the hands, neck and back. This means that touching is not necessarily an expression of a desire to change a person's mood to the better.

> *Never hinder a female from giving. This is a part of her nature and identity. A female gives endlessly on condition that she gets care and support. The female is an everlasting giving value.*

It is evident, then, that women who do not feel happy in their intimate sexual relationships with their partners are those who have lower oxytocin rates.

Kathleen Light; a professor of Psychological Medicine from North Carolina University, carried out studies on oxytocin rates in women. From her research, we come to know that "holding their partners' hands, having eye contact with and sleeping together, help women raise oxytocin rates in their bodies". This explains the charm of touching among lovers who spend long hours holding each other's hands. It also explains the secret of love by having mutual eye contact.

Researchers discovered that women who had happy intimate sexual relationships had higher oxytocin rates. Continuous researches show that some people have a natural genetic aptitude to develop higher oxytocin rates. They are the ones who can easily fall in love or get sexually aroused. Such people are unable of showing much resistance.

Researchers in Karolinska hospital in Sweden studied the effects of injecting oxytocin into the body and found out that a daily dose of this "cuddle and romance hormone" would reduce blood pressure and would stimulate a feeling of comfort and relaxation. That urged other researchers to believe that the intimate relationship may help people who have high blood pressure to get better or to be cured from some blood diseases such as leukemia.

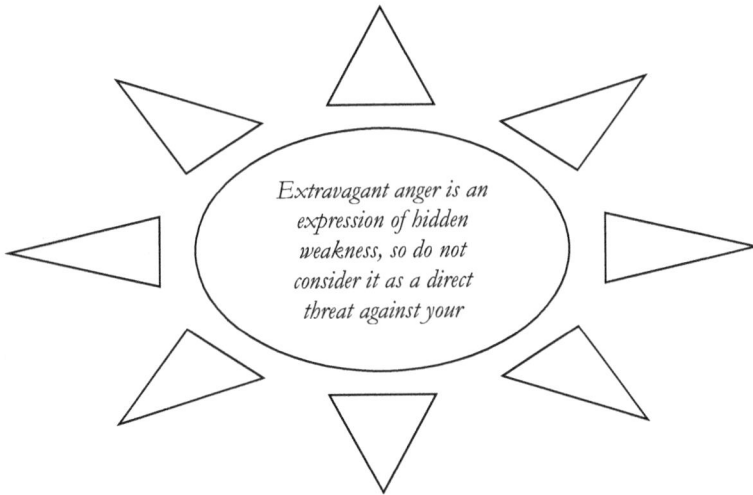

Extravagant anger is an expression of hidden weakness, so do not consider it as a direct threat against your

Dr. Legato finds a research supporting this vision made by David Wix; a psychiatrist at Edinburgh Royal Hospital. This researcher has found that spouses who have a sexual intercourse three times a week at least look 10 years younger than those who have it less. That can be
noticed on the faces of two lovers after having a romantic meeting where glamour and beauty that show on their faces are caused by this and other hormones.

Is Oxytocin Secretion the Same for Males and Females?

When the intimate sexual intercourse is over and satisfaction is realized, the cerebrum secretes oxytocin into the blood stream of both men and women equally, but as soon as the oxytocin meet the sex hormones there, its effects become extremely different, and it leads to completely different results. The estrogen in woman' blood enhances the effect of the oxytocin, reducing, thus, the blood pressure. She would feel happy and relaxed, and would develop a great desire to continue this connection by means o hugging, touching and talking. That is why she asks her partner to hug her and not to leave her after ejaculation.

> *Separate yourself from the criticism addressed to you and bear in mind that humor is the own secret of the permanent understanding you aspire to have.*

The testosterone in the male's bloodstream, on the other hand, which becomes higher during the sexual activity, neutralizes the oxytocin effect and reduces the desire to hug the female. This explains the male's desire, in most cases, to move away from his partner, and explains, in turn, her violent reaction to it as she thinks that he has got what he wants from her and then despised her!

While a woman wants to stay for a longer time with her partner to enhance the connection that has just happened, the man does not have a similar motive and is ready to move to anything else. This vision is enhanced by a study conducted by Dr. Light in the University of North Carolina on the oxytocin effects on blood pressure. There were no signs that men had higher oxytocin rates after massage. This might be attributed to the testosterone neutralizing effect of the oxytocin.

Love and Accompanying Signs of Sadness

Every one of us has probably realized that most great love affairs are characterized of pain and suffering, yet their heroes do not give up.

On the same issue, a research clarifies that parts of our minds paralyze when we love and that we feel distressed. This is, definitely, not a typical situation to take crucial decisions of change.

Our brains produce more dopamine to help us remain in high spirits in the face of crises. This is useful, but the feeling of serenity it creates might be fake. Now, we come to know the reason behind the calmness that follows cases of great sadness.

When this situation is over, the suprarenal gland "operates" the pituitary gland, which is the "factory" whereby all the hormones we need to survive a threat are made. The production of stimulating hormones like epinephrine and cortisol increases. This might be particularly harmful when the feeling of sadness remains for a very long time.

We realize what has just been mentioned when a love affair comes to an end. The result is that we will develop feelings of loneliness and terror similar to those we experienced when we were taken away from our mothers at a very early age. It is regaining of the pains of weaning and separation from those people whom we got familiar with the hormones of.

These views, which are presented in the light of the cogtive function of the masculine half, can, to some extent, explain the

biological side of love; the feminine side, to be more accurate
However, they will not be sufficient when it comes to considering
femininity as love. We present such views reservedly because we
are really convinced that they only provide a one-side explanation
which is, nevertheless, important. This, certainly, helps us
understand the mechanism according to which cerebrum of the
female works. It, consequently, helps us understand the female
herself.

Love and Understanding Will Not Last Forever

Happiness that accompanies love is temporary, hormonally
speaking, for there is no logic whatsoever in the constant secretion
of phenylethylamine and noradrenalin. No matter how high our
levels of hormones are especially in the first months or years of
love, our bodies still demand balance, therefore, those hormone
levels will, eventually, decrease. In the end, we will find ourselves
surrendering to some acts that might give a completely different
image from our reality. Yet, the question that arises in this context
is: "Are we supposed to be under the control of our hormones that
push us to be different? The answer might be *"YES"*. This is the
secret behind the wisdom that says: "**We cannot live happily
forever**"

The treatment that leads to production of the stimuli inducing
to cerebral communication and helps us have more understanding
through using both hemispheres can simply start with one of the
following means such as: laughing, exposing ourselves to sunshine,
waking up early, going on holiday, changing routine,
communicating with others, drinking alcohol, going dancing or
even making love. All this will, definitely, help us pass over the
traps set by our hormones since the latter cannot keep pushing us
towards happiness all the time.

Situated Behaviour

Different Change Strategies

The feminine mind deals with variables of life in a special way. We should note that a female has an inclination towards slow change. It is true that she tries to see the past off with deep consent, but she does not live it. This departure allows her to adopt a mechanism of slowness when heading towards new beginnings.

Her frequent slow actions are no more than a means of expressing the hesitation which actually characterizes the emotional aspect of her mental structure. As for the new starts, she tends to talk about them instead of going into them. She would visualize new things before turning them into real practice. However, this does not mean she does not enjoy affectionate flexibility towards the future.

She would stumble and sometimes she would get preoccupied in pre-thinking of alternatives. She would also like to have detailed images of the future before getting into it. Nonetheless, as soon as she starts the process of change, she will view the new facts from a completely unimaginable perspective to the extent that she might come up with innovative and unprecedented thoughts.

It is the nature of the feminine mind to be constantly based on emergence of ideas; i.e., thinking of what has never been thought of before on condition that such a change would give her the feeling of being secure.

What most characterizes the right cerebral hemisphere is coming up with genuine thoughts since it is in charge of all that is creative and qualitative in human life. Truly, we could have not achieved the innovative and creative ideas and works if intellectuals and inventors had not made use of the right cerebral hemisphere. In brief, without our feminine part, all humanity could have stayed in the stone ages.

The invention of the wheel, the Pyramids, building in dome style, discovery of the steam engine and feminine intuition altogether led to the emergence of Einstein's *"Theory of Relativity"*, thanks to the feminine mind of the masculine and feminine brains.

The male cannot understand the female's hesitation towards new circumstances before such circumstances turn to be realities. He tends to wrongly explain this situation by accusing the female of procrastination, inflexibility, and of being emotional and rash. Therefore, the occurrence of a tragic or disastrous event in the life of the female will assume changing stances because she does not follow the mechanism a male would follow in dealing with new situations. Thus, she needs time to forget and leave the past which occupies quite a large space of her right cerebral hemisphere. If the female, generally speaking, happens to be extremely talkative, she would need time to talk about that past and about the losses that event (change) has caused. However, the most important point is that as soon as change starts, it would be easier for a female to act creatively in the very process of change.

> *When you suggest something to a female and she refuses, this means that she is – somewhat – willing ... when she says "may be", this means she really wants it with all her heart. However, if she says "yes", be sure she is not a female because a female would never ever directly express what she wants.*

When a male is under pressure, he will get to his mind, as turtle would go inside its shell when it feels threatened. He would concentrate on solving the problem personally. Hence, he would choose the most persisting and most difficult problem of all and would concentrate on solving this problem only to the degree that he will temporarily be unaware of anything else. All other problems and responsibilities will be postponed; he is unilateral in dealing with changes. His full consciousness will not be present when dealing with all facts; he is more indulged in crises and changeable circumstances.

He keeps thinking and rethinking of his problem, which seems to have obsessed him, with the hope of finding a solution. In such a case, he will not be that competent in paying attention or considering feelings properly. He is entirely preoccupied with change and is not concerned but in accomplishing what he is working on. If he is unable of finding a solution to his problem, he will remain stuck whereas the female prefers to solve her problems via branching; i.e., sharing the problem with others so as to find a solution. She would go deep into the problem, see the pros and cons once and all over again. But, in the end, she will only do what she deems it right; she will act in accordance with her own viewpoint!

Again, we are in the course of discussing the purely feminine mind of a typical female or a few males whose feminine thinking has distinctively developed. The latter are not only those who are called "sissy", for there are others included.

Sometimes, during the formation process, the embryo could be subject to two high dosages of estrogen and testosterone at the same time which will result in the formation of an extraordinary masculine-feminine mind for the same person whether male or female. In fact, such people who possess such minds are the ones who are exceptionally creative!!!!!!

We should bear in mind that dissimilarities in the change strategies of males and females are partly derived from the affectionate masculine responses centralized in the right lobe while, in the case of females, they spread over the two lobes.

It is worth mentioning here that throughout the tension periods females undergo in their life, their bodies secrete the hormone of oxytocin which interacts with estrogen, thus, giving them the ability of social interaction and providing them with the possibility of being more involved in the process of change than males who start this process before females. However, during the tension periods which males undergo, they adopt a polarizing attitude; i.e., the attitude of (either…or) due to the hormone of testosterone which stimulates aggressive or defensive acts instead of digging up for compromising solutions.

> *Compliment the female for whatever work she does no matter how simple it is. This makes the female feel better when praised and increases her capability of giving endlessly whenever she is verbally boosted.*

The male is faster in launching change while the female is more capable of adapting herself to the hard times of the process of change. Hence, finding outlets at critical moments is a characteristic of the feminine mind, therefore, in such cases, males should listen to the female they bear inside or to their partner since she is the most competent of dealing with the strategies of change with deeper insight. Probably, a lot of males cannot soon comprehend that they really need the female's remarks. They need much time to realize how important such remarks are, but this is often realized when it is too late.

In actual reality, men violently and dually manage the change process of (either…or). Sometimes, women resist change hard, but the reasons behind such resistance are completely different from men's resistance which takes place at the very beginning. Women resist change due to hesitation and affectionate rejection to change while men resist due to their desire to remain attached to all what is static. That is to say, women resist out of fondness, intimate relatedness to a place and affectionate connection to the minute details about individuals while men resist out of fear of dealing with the unknown or fear of losing the determinants that allow control facts of the daily life.

Because the female makes use of the right cerebral hemisphere, she exercises affection, containment, multiplicity and cooperation; she is more capable of adapting to variables as regards the family affairs than the male. She is highly competent in finding alternatives as to provide her family members with care and patronage. Hence, we would not be telling a secret if we say that it has been proved that women who work outside the house; i.e., they have jobs that help them earn their living, and are fully in charge of all the chores and requirements of the house are the most capable of shouldering and carrying out such a doubled responsibility.

If the woman happens to be away from home and the man is left alone with the children or left to do the house chores, he would not be able to perform this task. In such societies, the absence of the husband will be problematic regarding the financial requirements or being the higher authority inside the house. However, the woman can work outside and shoulder the children's responsibility all along with carrying out the house requirements. She would do all this in a tremendously distinguished way if compared to the man who would feel confused if he is to have those very responsibilities (when he loses his wife for a reason or another). That is to say, the man will suffer from loss or inability to fulfill all tasks. He will not be as competent when communicating with his children as a woman does.

We focused, from the very beginning, on the female's capability of multiplicity, diversity, understanding and containment. The symbol of the female is *"the womb"*, i.e. containment, or rather, the warm containment that preserves life. Because she is the mother of male and female, she is capable of understanding, comprehending, containing and anticipating the behaviour of both of them, let alone her ability to get to know all that is going on inside each of them. The father, on the other hand, can only provide advice and get involved in work. However, he can provide his children with tenderness and compassion every now and then; nevertheless, he will turn later to be leader of the house and the higher authority.

The woman can reconcile working while assisting her elderly parents whereas the man tends to hire somebody to take care of them preferring to be overloaded with work in order to pay the costs of this service.

The masculine mind has an inclination to confront the change himself. The feminine mind, however, tends to involve others in this change especially when it comes to health changes. At this point, those who enjoy a masculine mind are not usually in favor of revealing their suffering as regards the change of their health condition whereas those enjoying a feminine mind would not apprehend confronting the change. Those with a feminine mind prefer to reveal their suffering and would like to share it with others especially those whom a female believes to sympathize with her, such as her beloved or her sons and daughters.

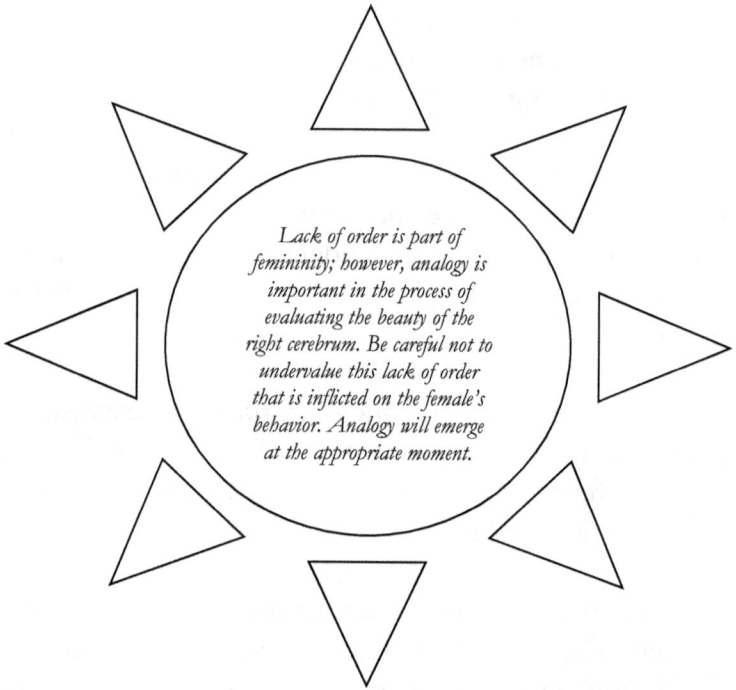

Lack of order is part of femininity; however, analogy is important in the process of evaluating the beauty of the right cerebrum. Be careful not to undervalue this lack of order that is inflicted on the female's behavior. Analogy will emerge at the appropriate moment.

During the change process, the feminine mind adopts the principle of *"exploration of the choices available"*, and *"the maneuver technique"* away from huge losses. The feminine mind accepts the principle of *"negotiation"* and, to some extent, *"bargains and concessions"* with the purpose of avoiding any negative dramatic results. The male's strategy, on the other hand, is different. A male would adopt the technique of controlling and holding mechanisms, with the intention of evading enormous losses, but the excessive implementation of this strategy will probably lead to worse consequences due to lack of flexibility.

Since following the *"necessity of choice"* principle while running the process of change is a characteristic of the feminine mind, we come to know that the prominent leaders of the world who succeeded in managing grave crises were not those having strong will, firmness and good tactics because of the masculine mind they enjoyed. On the contrary, great leaders of the world were those who could utilize their feminine mind as to discover ways out, reduce losses and have the ability to bring about alternatives, negotiate and reach compromises. Therefore, they were able of widening the circle of choice at the time of having difficulty, thus, they could avoid the option of (either...or). To wrap up, the preeminent successful leadership manifests by seizing the opportunity of moving from the strategy of "either...or" to the strategy of "both...and".

Going back to history, we realize that the losing leaders were those who confined their attitudes to the dichotomy of: (To be or not to be). The winners, however, were those who subjugated circumstances to their own will. They adapted themselves to incidents and did not deal with them from their own perspectives. They dealt with possibilities to be able to reach the appropriate time to attack their enemies. The most momentous historic stage was when men were able to achieve peace of the brave, i.e. the peace which cannot be achieved by the masculine mentality of "either...or"; rather, by utilizing the feminine mind. Within the strategies of change, the feminine mind does not confine itself to one or (maximum) two options. It searches for the best of a diversity of options, thus, *"the necessity of choice"* imposes itself as a feminine feature at a dramatic moment.

To recapitulate, the mechanisms of change confrontation of a male manifest in quick action while, in the case of a female, they manifest in deep thinking, looking for details and consultation. Therefore, the masculine change technique is successful only when a prompt and instantaneous action is required. However, if the change results are not clear and there is time to think deeply and thoroughly of a miscellany of options, the feminine approach will be more successful. Hesitation and contemplation will not be characteristics of change if the female is not attached to the past. In other words, when the female's evaluation of the current situation or the past is negative, the best way to convince her of the new circumstances; *"variables"*, will be through spotting the negative points of the past; a mechanism that destroys her typical mechanism; i.e. *"nostalgia"*.

It is wise to keep the female involved in the past since it is her nature to feel nostalgic. However, she should not be left to indulge and drown herself completely in that past because this will make her abstain from change. Her partner has to give her a hand when she is in such a situation by spotting the positive points of the coming change or future that resembles what she feels nostalgic for. But, he has to bear in mind that his aid should not appear as a kind of sympathy with that nostalgia. The first step toward acceptance of changes is embodied in the process of preparing her to acknowledge the sentimental losses resulting from the conditions of change. This cannot be attained unless the new conditions are not in conflict with her type of feeling.

The most important stage that confirms the female's access into change is the attempt to step over the transitional stages; i.e. between nostalgia to the past and the new condition. This undoubtedly means *the necessity of reaching that stage as soon as possible.* It is a period of moving from the old to the new. It is critical and uncomfortable, and is characterized by the possibility of deterioration. Attempting to control such a period seems to be quite difficult, therefore, in order not to regress to the past, the female has to quit it as quickly as possible.

* * * * * *

Better Your Life ...

1.   Stop criticism.

2.   Learn to accept each other.

4.Do not give negative interpretations for the motives behind what your partner says or does.

5.Bear in mind that you are not always on the side of angels. The truth is the one which opposite is a truth as well. Truths are our convictions; they are not objects or absolutes.

6.Stop holding to your belief that you are better and more knowledgeable than your partner. If you are a real man-of-knowledge, try to share this knowledge with others not to play the role of the instructor.

7.Act justly all the time.

8.Do not apply the rule of "wrestling of wills". Substitute it with "sharing of wills".

9.Remember that life means "taking and giving"; however, it will be far better if you change the order to be "giving and taking".

10. Avoid having a narcissistic character.

11. You have to recall that imposing your opinion upon your partner means that the latter is going to either impose their opinion publicly (this will result in **a direct collision** between you), or they are going to impose it secretly which means (**your separation**).

12. Do not count on miracles to sweep your problems away. Fast solutions do only exist in myths. Therefore, you have to bear in mind that you are dealing with a human being; not with an illusion.

13. Do not think you can change anyone. Human beings have already been formed the way they are. You cannot replace their way of living with one you yourself make because you will project your own personality and the rest will be made by life.

14. Do not consider the partner's attempts to change you as a threat. Just have self-confidence and tell yourself that those (already failing) attempts are a sign of love and a desire to be together forever. Your partner's attempts are demands you have to take into consideration so as to get what is positive and appropriate.

15. Enjoy tranquility which is far more important than calm. Do not be rash or impatient because life does not approve such edgy people.

16. No one whosoever can be a god. You are not perfect.

17. Do not make openness to the other a chance to insult your partner.

18. Stop arguing over irresolvable problems or problems you do not have the key to solve. If the other party insists on talking about them, listen carefully without agitation. Show real interest by sympathizing with your

partner and calmly admitting that you cannot (now) find a way out but you promise you will (even if this seems to be almost impossible).

19. Disparities and diversities in the minds and moods of people are part and parcel of nature. Therefore, it is good to feel the grace of disparity.

20. Soothe the situation that is too serious. Having succeeded, add a sense of humor, **but** you have to take care not to take such an action from the outset lest the other party feel you are undervaluing what they say.

21. Read the hidden intents lying behind all the thoughts or accusations addressed by the other. However, do not act like a detective or a susceptible obsessive person. Only try to uncover the real reason through deep thinking and understanding the motives and reasons. Such actions might be motivated by love, foil, a desire to have further communication (through negative expressions) or a desire to achieve a special position that is already threatened.

22. Do not get into quarrels over trivialities; such trivialities reveal the deeply-hidden things in our psychology.

23. Change the course of the dialogue with your partner from the beginning and try not to forget yourself in the dialogue problems.

24. Learn to use expressions like: "I am sorry. I will try to have a better consideration of the issue next time".

25. Use the position of the upper pyramid by putting your hands in this situation in front of your chest because they will prevent the other from exceeding the limits or offending you.

26. Help the other party mitigate the impact of a hot debate between you.

27. Mitigate your internal agitation and bear in mind that it occurs due to biological, physiological or hormonal reasons that have nothing to do with the issue of discussion.

28. Abdominal breathing is recommended, but try not allow your chest expand more than your belly while discussions.

29. Watch your thoughts; i.e., think of your own thinking.

30. If you feel you have high blood pressure, stop talking immediately because you are not up to hold a sound or healthy discussion neither healthily nor mentally.

31. Do not end the discussion you are having with your partner; only ask for postponing it. Do not give direct answers. Try to maneuver. In this way, you give yourself and the other party the opportunity to have deep positive thinking.

32. Do not allow a third party to interfere in any of you and your partner's discussions or conflicts because this will lead to triplet emotional and polemic discussions which will, in turn, aggravate the problems.

33. Renounce the language of dissatisfaction. Use a language of forgiveness and remission and remember that *to forgive* means to let a situation or the word go for a while, but you restore it later on because it has a deep internal effect. *To remit*, however, means to turn the page of past actions with no impact left whatsoever. Anyway,

both of you should exempt the other. If it is not the case, be the one who takes the initiative.

34. Stop ruminating the past because you are currently living in the present and tomorrow is the future. In addition, there is no connection between past, present and future but in your own mind. If you are the type who restores the past that heavily, try to make this recur at a minimum and learn to put an end to such a recall at the end of the day.

35. Put an end to dialogue inhibitors which lie in the excessive expectations pinned on the other. Bear in mind ... No provocative conversations ... No urgent demands ... No frowning ... No tension ... No high stern tone used ... No underestimation of the feelings of the other ... No contempt ... No reiteration of childish, patriarchal or instructive words or comments ... No passing of quick rash judgments ... No partial listening nor listening superficially without getting the gist ... Let your smile be your first step towards the other.

36. Quit double standards and the idea that you are entitled to do what others are not entitled to.

37. Do not take obsessive attitudes.

38. Reproach lovingly. Do not do reproach out of defending yourself or attacking the other.

39. Instill confidence in your partner.

40. Raise the compliment dose and remember that since "compliment" and "complete" have the same root, they come to mean that both parties complete each other and are in need of one another.

41. Boost the dreams and aspirations of your partner at least by words if you were not able to achieve them by actions.

42. Your partner is not your rival. Therefore, always give them a loving and passionate look. This is highly recommended.

43. Dignity should have no place in your relationship with your partner if you want to have an elegant and permanent relationship. Be sure that the other is not "*The Hell*".

44. The other is not a subject or a piece of dough that can be changed easily. The other is an individual who has been formed in their time and their own society and have had their own experiences. Your relationship with the other is nothing but exchange of experiences and interaction between your own individualities.

45. Never ever think that your partner is the worst when they outburst. There might be a worse partner whom you have not met yet. Bear in mind that you have a good partner with bad circumstances.

46. While reacting to your partner's complaints, avoid reminding them of your favors and how much you have offered. They are quite aware of this. Maybe they want more, or they want something qualitative at that very moment.

47. Any trouble in the world is caused by two not one person. Therefore, you have to ask yourself about your very acts that caused that problem.

48. The male has his own language, so does the female. Hence, the moment you feel that your partner does not understand you, be sure that you are using your own subjective language not his or hers. If you immediately use or switch to their language, you will be surprised at the results you will have[*].

49. Avoid correcting your partner while they are talking. Do not say: "Yes, but..." because it will not give the results you aspire to have. Instead, you can say: "Yes, I am convinced that you are well-aware of so and so". Your partner might not be aware of what you are saying, but once you say such words, you will urge them to have a sense of their own selves and superego; something which will, definitely, lead to a mutual understanding between you both.

50. A male has to understand the motives of the female's outburst before and during her menstrual period. Premenstrual syndromes (PMS) come out of a severe drop of estrogen

51. accompanied with pain, impatience and quick outburst. A has to know that those very symptoms create life; thus, they are a prerogative of the female.

52. Learn how to have a language that involves "a common vision", not the language of "imposition". The common vision makes your partner a party, not just a mere passer-by.

53. Be careful not to make your partner feel that your mutual life might end up coincidentally just as it began. You

---

[*] See "How a Female Thinks" to understand the language of the female and differentiate it from that of the male.

should make use of the language of (forever) which makes both partners feel secure.

54. Do not ever warn your partner, for you are not a policeman.

55. Try to change your negative attitude towards your partner's behavior. Use a means of a positive transfer. For example, you can consider your partner's jealousy as something irritating and restricting; however, you can see it as an evidence of great love. The former view is destructive while the latter is constructive.

56. Express your ideas accurately. No one would ever figure out what is going on in your mind. However, a male has to know that it is hard for a female to express her own ideas simply because she wants her male to understand her right away and from the first sign. Only this will prove his love towards her.

57. Step over trivialities. Do not be like an archeologist excavating disturbing details.

58. Allow your partner some freedom. Do not let them feel they are monitored or they have no will.

59. Do not ever embarrass your partner in front of others. If you do so, you will drive them to think of getting rid of you because their image has been deformed. Your partner does not live only with you; they live with others and nourish their being from their image which is depicted in people's minds.

60. Let tranquility overwhelm you and remember that it is tranquility that makes you relax, live in peace and take right decisions. Only people of tranquility can enjoy a

peaceful life. They are a special kind of leaders, quoted everywhere.

61. Do not make of a problem a major one. Apply your circuit on a parallel basis where if you have a failure somewhere, your life does not break down completely. Do not let your partner shoulder the burden of your problems and do not consider that one problem with them is the devil itself.

62. When you feel your partner is embittering your life, try to please them. Only those who feel happy can impart happiness on others.

63. Put your work trouble aside the moment you step into your house as if you were taking off your clothes. No one inside the house is responsible for what is outside but you.

64. Stop using the language of (internal/external) and do not be skeptical about the motives. You will never get into the depths. The other is not a conspirator. They are probably not.

65. Do not expect the other to meet your ultimate demands. Expect on the basis of what they are expected to do.

66. Accept apology with love and modesty, not with superiority and triumph.

67. Odd behavior might look like insanity or genius. View them as genius, for they can bestow happiness upon your life.

68. When you doubt the other…. wait!

69. For a relationship to survive, there should be no conditions. Make your relationship a grant without conditions, for a relationship based on conditions is almost a contract that can be annulled. Relationship without any conditions whatever is an everlasting contract of love.

70. Do not compare your partner neither implicitly nor explicitly, and neither before them nor before others. No one is perfect. No one can be a god. The demerits of the one you do not know are much more than your partner's. Hence, it is better not to venture the unknown.

71. Be proud of your partner. At least, remember that you have chosen them out of millions of people. You must have hit the bull's eye.

72. Make use of your intuition not your premonition. Learn that intuition and feeling are highly interrelated.

73. Do not say "No." Learn to say it in a way that does not make the other feel rejected.

74. Do not feel guilty and do not make your partner feel guilty, either.

75. Pay attention to the other to make them calm down. Never ignore them.

76. The female has to give the male the chance to stay in his cave as long as he wishes. She does not have to urge him to communicate or ask him a lot of questions.

77. Partners do not have to compete to obtain the approval of one another.

78. Maintain mutual trust.

79. Avoid telling lies because they constitute the way that leads to mistrust accumulation. It could be a one-way ticket.

80. A post-conflict kiss can stop conflict recurrence.

81. Never feel you are a victim. This feeling kills you both.

82. Do not compare your work and responsibilities to those of your partner's. Each should act according to their own abilities. No one has to be like the other.

83. Compliment the female for whatever work she does no matter how simple it is. This has two implications. This first is that the female feels better when praised and the second is that her capability of giving increases endlessly whenever she is verbally boosted.

84. Support your words with deeds, and remember that the female is an auditory creature. She is extremely sensitive and very cautious lest she is deceived.

85. After a hard day of work, a female would adapt to the Animus, for daily work often needs utilizing the left cerebral hemisphere. Therefore, she needs time and effort as to regain herself and her feminine. The access can be through sentiments and feelings.

86. Everything the female asks the male to do or bring will lose value. Things get value only when the male gets his female what she does not ask for; i.e., when he estimates what she is in need of. The female would not approve requesting the male at all, for this will be a real admission of the male's ingratitude which her femininity never accepts.

87. It is not necessary that every negatively answered question by a female means "No", for this could be an attempt to urge you raise further questions, to protest against being not cared for, to tell her that you understand her without verbal expression, or to take action without her requesting you. In all cases, she says "yes" and protests by "No". Remember that when a female says "No", she means "perhaps", and when she says "perhaps", she means "yes", but when she says "yes", this means she is *NOT* a female.

88. You should avoid the direct questions of a female when she is provoked. She is in a state of catharsis or discharging negative energy, so do not let her escalate. Let her continue raising questions and reply her briefly or listen carefully. Be careful not to maneuver or use her indirect way of talking.

89. The female's mind is formulated in such a way as to receive which is a starting point to giving. She is extremely concerned about details and she adores gifts whatever their value is. She is so keen on communication and feeling the other's caring for her. Bringing her a valuable gift once in a while is fine; however, bringing her gifts every now and then even if they are not very precious will please her. The measure here is based on quality not quantity.

90. Be aware of dealing with a female while she is in the regular period. The lower rates of estrogen imply an increase of testosterone. This stimulates extreme aggressiveness, and means having illogical discussions. It arises in her sexual desire, but it causes her depression. Do not argue with her in such a period. She lies on the opposite side to her nature. The male inside her (testosterone) is higher than the female (estrogen). Her body and mind are turned upside down.

91. The female is in need of full support in order to keep in touch with the feminine side which has decreased with the decrease of estrogen. Such a situation will unconsciously recall the feminine side of the male (tenderness, warmth, love, weakness....etc). Even though, it is important not to exaggerate in playing the female's role after that because women do not favor weak men. They love those who encompass them with tenderness at this specific time of the regular period.

92. Most artists and poets are distinguished with their exceptional right cerebral hemisphere. Thus, their exaggeration of their feminine needs is so prominent. They are most capable of drawing the attention to their beauty. At the beginning, the female will be enchanted since they fulfill part of her femininity. But, realizing femininity happens only with fully masculine men. Therefore, you have to be careful when you have that flow of feminine sentiments.

93. Be careful not to request the female to be your mother, sister, girlfriend and beloved. She only has one job, and she will never ever be your mother. She will not respect that male who holds to his mother. You might assume that your love to your mother will complement her love and that she will appreciate it and consider it as a guarantee to her love. This does not work. She thinks in a completely different way. She does not respect the man who has not been weaned yet.

94. The balance you strike between your masculinity and femininity will urge her to respect and love you.

95. When the female is not in harmony with her very nature as a female; i.e., when she does excessive masculine work or when she undergoes sharp decrease of estrogen,

she tries to have many biological practices so as to balance her psychological situation. In such a case, the male should not blame her for this tendency. He should bring her back to the field of femininity through sentimental practices and through indulging her in feminine affiliations along with sharing part of her burden.

96. The female, who is indulged in the masculine life requests the male to be gentler and more delicate when dealing with her. In fact, she is demanding herself of that through him. Therefore, do not be harsh with her; assist her through containing and sympathizing with her to help her reveal her femininity, softness and delicacy. Beware of being looked at as a female, and at the same time do not be harsh and offensive.

97. The female's misery is a result of being indulged. She indulges in emotional interaction with several issues all at once, which confuse her. So, do not blame her. She is not biologically prepared to deal with issues separately. She deals with things collectively not individually. You have to remember that females do not feel at ease when they perform masculine activities. Hence, their only way of expressing that is through their non-stop and constant narration of their problems until they release what is in their inside.

98. A female has a tendency towards looking as oppressed. She has an unconscious belief that she will not obtain sympathy unless the others feel she is made unjust and is badly treated. Do not forget this when you deal with her exaggeration of being a victim of the feeling of injustice. However, when she finds nobody to listen to her complaint, she will shrink and launch self –destructive actions such as self-torment self-impeachment, and making ultimate

judgments against herself. In this case, she aims at punishing the other throughout punishing herself.

99. It is a natural characteristic of a female that she does not ask for help; however, she gets upset when the male does not offer that help. Therefore, you ought to examine and guess what her needs, and then act in response to her undeclared demands.

100. Notice that the female gives constantly, nevertheless, she waits for your giving in order to recharge hers. The biggest mistake a male would commit is when he imagines that he is dealing with a god who gives persistently and silently because this god does not want the giving of others. So, avoid the explosion of those who silently give and you do not even think of rewarding.

101. When a female does not make use of women's language, do not imagine that she is satisfied with this masculine image, no matter how much self assurance and satisfaction she expresses for competing men and occupying a prominent position in males' world. She is living in contrast to her identity. No matter how much satisfaction her position brings her; she has nostalgia to be the centre of males' care and love unlike some women who undergo confusions in their sexual identity due to hormonal causes.

102. Every female is a unique creature from her point of view. Her narcissism does not give the chance for anyone to compare her to any other female in the whole universe. Be careful not to compare her to any female; do not ask her to be a copy of any other model. The most dangerous of all is when you demand her to be a duplicate of an ex-female you have met in your life.

103. The more you praise her personal characteristics the more you enhance those attributes. Do not persist or criticizing her negative aspects. Overlook her negative sides by enhancing and occasionally exaggerating her positive sides. This is the key to dealing with the inherent negative aspects of her structure and character.

104. Do not raise her jealousy unless she is a masochist. The masochist female is fond of the male who ignores her and insults her femininity through jealousy or betrayal. It is a part of self-torturing mechanism. A non-masochist female is narcissistic and is concerned about her femininity as previously mentioned. However, some phallic women; women experiencing castration complex, occasionally exaggerate their feminine reaction against jealousy or betrayal through excessive verbal violence or excessive hostility under the title of "dignity". Females commonly feel tranquility with those who afford them reassurance and appreciate their femininity.

105. Do not prevent female from crying. She releases her tension by crying. You have to know that the female who has excessive fits of crying is the most feminine. This type is contrary to the masculine female who does not prefer to cry in order not to be accused of weakness.

106. Sexual interaction is not favorable and inappropriate at her extreme anger or emotion unless she is a masochist. A non-masochist female does not like having sex if she is irritated. Never interrupt her desire through discussing any other issue that necessitates thinking nor blame her for any behavior. Do not insult her femininity because this will instantly bring her desire to a halt.

107. The female is constantly in need of those who elevate her feeling of eternal youth and everlasting beauty.

Bearing in mind that there is no ugly woman on earth; each woman has her own particular beauty in a specific aspect. The beauty of woman could not be perfect excluding very rare cases, thus, boost her feeling of her own beauty, get her assured and point to her beauty persistently. This will help her put an end to any feeling related to her identity crisis.

108. All fashions promote the female's tendency to nakedness through the binary opposition of "exterior-interior"; i.e., disclosing part of the body while concealing another part which incites seduction. This is part of the female's natural choice of clothes; however, this is accompanied with a paradox: the female desires to expose her full or semi nakedness, but she will be uncomfortable if she does not feel her male's jealousy over her. She herself makes it for public in her own way and to whoever she decides. She wants to show it, but not to sell it.

109. You should recognize the tremendous care a female allots to her skin. Her skin equals her; it is her identity and the front façade. The skin is what body of the female wears. It is not merely a mirror to her emotions. It is the wall that protects her internal depth. Hence, incessant mutual touching is a way of reviving her relation with her body.

110. Accusing a female of having an inclination towards deceiving is true and untrue at the same time. She resorts to the technique of maneuver and gets away from the yes/no or either/or techniques. She revolves around her issues, thus, she looks like a deceiver. Beware of being convinced that she is really deceitful. She is mysterious because of her feminine structure. So, try to read what she refuses to declare; behave accordingly.

111. Every female; deep in her unconscious considers herself as symbol of the utmost femininity. Therefore, when she falls in love, she would yearn to embalm her beloved to keep him for herself only. She would surround him and would even wish not to allow him meet or deal with any other female.

Index

www.ingramcontent.com/pod-product-compliance
Lightning Source LLC
Chambersburg PA
CBHW071030280326
41935CB00011B/1515